a guide for finding your place in the world

THE EMERGING
SENSITIVE

MARIA HILL

Printed in the United States of America

First Printing, 2016

Print ISBN 978-1-68222-474-8
eBook ISBN 978-1-68222-475-5

Bookbaby
7905 N. US-130,
Pennsauken Township, NJ 08110

www.bookbaby.com

To my husband, Rod, for his support and to my sensitive
cat and muse, Kelly!

TABLE OF CONTENTS

PREFACE

I am a highly sensitive person who has grappled with being sensitive my whole life. I believe that all HSPs do. I also think that each highly sensitive person uses the trait as a point of departure to investigate aspects of the world that are intriguing, mysterious, or confounding.

My investigations began with my family whose ultra conservative values, goals, interests, and expectations I did not understand or relate to. Like a lot of highly sensitive women, I did not like sexism either. As a child I was confused by the world. It seemed to make so many people unhappy and my efforts to change the unhappiness around me met with little success.

I seemed to approach everything differently. I noticed and listened to energy, which meant I had difficulty connecting with other people in a way that they expected. I took in all of the expressed and unexpressed energy around me, which was confusing and overwhelming. Even at age six, I scratched my head until it bled sometimes because I was so confused by the people around me. I was already contemplative at a young age.

One thing that I found strange was the expectations. My parents were demanding but I noticed a problem with their expectations. Their expectations had little to do with what an individual could do, what they had time to do, or the process needed to get something done. Their expectations seemed to be enough for them and not enough for me. I also noticed how living from expectations resulted in poor planning and therefore resources problems and obstacles would be overlooked. These issues made good work difficult and less enjoyable and created a lot of conflicts.

Expectations were a big part of the challenge I had. When I examined them energetically, I discovered that most expectations are stagnant, which did not make sense to me since the world is always changing. Fixed expectations leave little room for growth and development, and

I found that very difficult to live with. The world is a dynamic place and fixed expectations are not a dynamic way of relating to life and the world.

I am a creative person—a writer and abstract painter. I have always approached everything from a creative perspective. Being creative is natural to me. However, to many people around me, creativity carried a negative charge and some treated it as a form of rebellion. Whether in my family, church, or school, creativity was disparaged.

I have an inside-out way of working—I approach life from what needs to be done. I like doing good work and that requires that you ask yourself what the work needs, not what everyone else wants. When you put the work first, it can seem to others that you are being adversarial when you are not.

The fixed and angry ideology I experienced in my early years caused me to want to discover the reasons why my family and the world were the way they were. I kept looking for some flow and found myself bumping into walls. I knew that the world keeps changing and wondered why my family would not. I wanted to learn new things, discover different ways of thinking, and my family's minds were closed. I wanted to open windows and they kept shutting doors. Eventually I had to go my own way and pursue my learning on my own without their support. It was a decision that I had to make, but it left me sad.

I have spent many years educating myself —both formally and informally— as well as working in a variety of environments, including health care and the computer industry to learn more about the world and how it works. My perception has always been that life does not have to be as unhappy as it often is. I do not believe that people have to be as alienated from each other as they often seem to be.

I know I am not alone in the feelings of alienation and disconnection that I have experienced as a highly sensitive person. I have been looking for answers and found some very useful ones in frameworks that help me understand how people become who they are and how cultures work, and now I understand what I could not understand as a child. It has brought me peace and new hope that in learning patterns we can apply our creativity and insight into constructive approaches for relating and problem solving.

I am passing on what I have learned with the hope it helps other highly sensitive people have an easier time coming to terms with all of the different perspectives and energies they encounter in the world.

ACKNOWLEDGEMENTS

I wish to personally thank the following people for their contributions to my inspiration and knowledge and other help in creating this book:

- My family for providing me with endless food for thought

- Dr. Elaine Aron whose groundbreaking work has given highly sensitive people a way of understanding themselves

- All of the wonderful people serving the highly sensitive community from whom I learn every day

- Other highly sensitive people whose generous hearts and many kindnesses make our world more livable than they can know

- My editors: Cara Benson of GrubStreet whose empathy, perspective, insights and questions helped make this a better book. Samantha Gordon of Invisible Ink Editing for polishing the book so that it was much more readable.

- John Morad and the designers of Bookbaby for bringing the book to life.

INTRODUCTION

Hundreds of highly sensitive people (HSPs) have told me about their yearning to live fuller lives. They feel left out, distrusted, and at a loss for how to make a place for themselves in the world.

HSPs suffer from complicated challenges. Some of the greatest needs of highly sensitive people are safety and a belief that they can find a place in the world for themselves. Highly sensitive people often feel unwanted and without a social home because they are outsiders. As a result, they live with an unwelcome absence of place, which comes from just being who they are.

Some challenges of highly sensitive people are easier to handle than others. For example, stress levels are something a large number of HSPs learn to manage early on. Many of us know that we must slow down, take good care of our health, meditate, and reduce stress as much as possible. Even if we do all those things, we have no guarantee of the life we imagine and truly deserve. Goals like finding suitable work and relating to non-HSPs can be difficult to realize. We are different creatures. The world has not accepted us—yet!

The good news is that the world is changing, albeit slowly, and we now have the opportunity to take our place. This book will help you understand the special times we live in and embrace a well-deserved opportunity to become a part of the world. I hope it offers you a new vision for what is possible for you.

Being sensitive does not mean having purely soft, gentle feelings, although tender and empathetic feelings are an important hallmark of highly sensitive natures. HSPs have a unique nervous system, which takes in the complexity of the world, and as a result we can easily notice lots of unmet needs and want to address them. Because of our humanitarian instincts, we often focus on ignored issues in the world, which can make us seem like troublemakers.

When we evaluate ourselves by the embraced values of Western culture, we have a hard time situating ourselves in a world that devalues sensitivity. As a result, we may have difficulty discovering a positive vision and path for ourselves.

The challenges facing highly sensitive people are so complex that finding a way to make sense of it can be daunting. Highly sensitive people are gifted but often do not receive the support they need to bring their gifts into the world. The purpose of this book is to help highly sensitive people understand themselves better, come to terms with their outsider status in a positive way, find a new path for themselves that will work, and create joy.

The book is divided into four parts:

- **Part 1: Understanding The Highly Sensitive Trait:**
  - » The biological difference of highly sensitive people and the implications of that difference physically, emotionally, and experientially.

  - » The 'DOES' Model Of Highly Sensitive People created by Dr. Elaine Aron, which defines the key ways highly sensitive biology results in different ways of thinking and processing information for highly sensitive people.

- **Part 2: The Importance And Value Of Frameworks:**
  - » What frameworks are, why they are important and how they help us make sense of the world better.

  - » The evolution framework, the insights it offers highly sensitive people and how it can be used to make processing information easier.

- **Part 3: Getting A Handle On The World:**
  - » The structural reasons you feel out of sync with the world and find it hard to thrive.

» How the world is changing and why it provides fresh opportunities for highly sensitive people that will make life more fulfilling.

» New fields and opportunities for highly sensitive people to do work that suits their natures.

- **Part 4: Claiming Agency:**

  » What is "agency" and why is it hard to claim agency as a highly sensitive person.

  » Skills and tools that highly sensitive people need to harness their sensitivity for positive results

  » Questions to ask to start investigating new possibilities for your life.

- Resources by section to help you investigate new ideas, opportunities, and skills.

I hope you find the book uplifting and helpful.

PART 1: THE HIGHLY SENSITIVE TRAIT

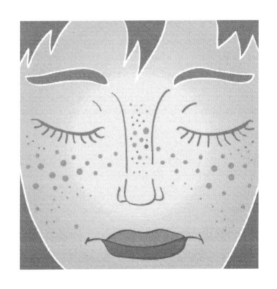

Highly sensitive people have always existed, but little has been known about them. This section explores the biological difference of highly sensitive people. It explains the impact of HSP biology and explores the research findings of Dr. Elaine Aron and others into the nature and manifestation of the highly sensitive trait by focusing on Dr. Aron's "DOES" model as a framework for understanding the most important characteristics of highly sensitive people.

CHAPTER 1

The Fundamental Difference Of Highly Sensitive People

Highly sensitive people absorb the energy around them like a sponge. Working with that energy in a positive and constructive way is the foundation for their life journey. Where many people form identities primarily from factors like sex, race, religion, and social or occupational roles, HSPs identify first with their energy-oriented nature and the natural world. You could say that energy is their home.

In 1996, Dr. Elaine Aron published her groundbreaking book, The Highly Sensitive Person. In it, she detailed the special nature of the highly sensitive person, which she attributed to genetic causes. What this means is that through no fault of their own and because of a biological inheritance, a highly sensitive person has a different nervous system and is therefore biologically different from other people.

One out of five people is highly sensitive, a trait that exists in humans and more than 100 other species. Most highly sensitive people are introverted but approximately 30% of HSPs are extroverted. Highly sensitive people have always existed but until recently have been characterized as anything from misfits to madmen to geniuses to saints. Grappling with the labels people ascribe to HSPs can be overwhelming and confusing. Phew!

The confusion of the general population about the nature of highly sensitive people, and the myriad ways popular culture has addressed the issue, has historically made it difficult for HSPs to develop a clear mental image of themselves. Thanks to Dr. Aron's pioneering work, that is changing. Highly sensitive people are emerging from the shadows and the genius of the highly sensitive person is making its way onto the human stage.

Highly sensitive people have been at odds with their world for an important reason: HSPs cannot avoid feeling in a world that suppresses feeling. Highly sensitive people who have a nervous system that acts like a sponge cannot avoid what their nervous system brings to them. They absorb all the energy around them.

The world marches to mental models of life, which describe "how it is." Some such models include how men and women are, what aging is like, etc. Highly sensitive people approach the world differently. Because of the finely tuned receptivity of their nervous systems and their energetic connection with the world, highly sensitive people cannot be stuck on the mental plane because their bodies are built differently and do not allow it. In a way, HSPs are much more in touch with reality than others as long as they can sort out all the information they receive.

Energy is complete information. Highly sensitive people, because of their biology, bring new perceptual information and possibilities to the world from which they get the energy they take in, which causes them to have exceptional empathy, sensitivity to nuance, conscientiousness, deep processing, and creativity. They are often visionaries and can become gifted healers and artists.

The HSP's unique experience of the world is extremely valuable but misunderstood and therefore not put to use in a thoughtful and effective manner. As a result, highly sensitive people experience more vulnerability than non-HSPs—this includes feeling the vulnerability of those around them. For many HSPs, being different makes it hard to reveal and celebrate the special gifts of their sensitivity.

Sensitivity, though painful at times, can become an important path to wisdom. Although being highly sensitive can make relationships, work, and self-care difficult, the abundant information that highly sensitive people can access and process offers the potential for important insights and creative breakthroughs. The challenge for highly sensitive people is to embrace the vulnerability their nature creates in a way that helps them become more skilled and effective in life. There are risks, however.

Risks For Highly Sensitive People
Highly sensitive people face some serious risks to their well-being:

- The tempo of an aggressive, automated society is a no-go for HSPs. Only those with strong support systems and exceptional personal productivity can survive modern work environments.

- Some people value empathy and others do not. Being aware of who you are dealing with can help you avoid becoming invested in individuals who are incompatible and devaluing of your nature.

- Being different can mean social isolation, making it difficult to create a rewarding social life.

- The world is organized to support non-HSPs, so sensitive people have to be careful to choose medical and other support from people receptive to the highly sensitive trait and willing to treat it with respect.

Finally and most importantly, HSPs need to develop their own internal definition of success in a world that is driven by external values, because otherwise they can feel buffeted by the values and agendas of others.

The Biggest Difference Between HSPs and Non-HSPs

All humans are social creatures, however highly sensitive natures do not manifest in the same way as those of non-sensitive people. Non-HSPs are more likely extroverted and emphasize the culturally approved rewards of life as a primary driver for the way they live. HSPs are social creatures as well but are energy-sensitive. A study by Dr. Arthur Aron and his colleagues has shown that highly sensitive people are not as influenced by culture:

> Our data suggest that some categories of individuals, based on their natural traits, are less influenced by their cultural context than others," says Dr. Aron. He adds that the study is the first to analyze how a basic temperament/personality trait, called sensory processing sensitivity (SPS), interacts with culture and neural responses...

> The researchers measured SPS in 10 East Asian individuals temporarily in the U.S. and 10 Americans of Western-European ancestry. In a previous study, these same 20 individuals had undergone brain functional magnetic resonance imaging (fMRI) while performing a cognitive task of comparing the length of lines inside boxes. The participants' responses to the task tested their perception of the independence versus interdependence of objects as the fMRI measured the neural basis of their responses...

> In the SPS study, Dr. Aron and colleagues took the brain activations in these two groups from the previous study and considered them in light of the SPS scores of the same individuals. They found SPS as a trait yielded a very clear pattern of results:

"The influence of culture on effortful perception was especially strong for those who scored low on the scale measuring sensitivity, but for those who scored high on the measure (highly sensitive individuals), there was no cultural difference at all," says Dr. Aron. Regarding the fMRI, Dr Aron adds: "Culture did not influence the degree of activation of highly sensitive individuals' brains when doing the two kinds of perceptual tasks used in the previous study. Also, how much they identified with their culture had no effect. It was as if, for them, culture was not an influence on their perception."

Dr. Aron emphasized that the new research suggests that characteristics possessed by high SPS individuals, such as being emotionally reactive or conscientious, actually flow out of or are side effects of the overriding feature of processing information more thoroughly than low SPS individuals. [1]

Because HSP nervous systems pick up energy and are constantly processing energy, they do not take their cues from the culture as much from the energy in their environment. For a highly sensitive person, energy is information and the focus of their attention.

Being energy sensitive means HSPs are exposed to all of the energy in their environment, which include current issues and concerns, conscious and unconscious energy, and all present and suppressed emotions in the people around them. They work to understand the energy and let it inform them in their decisions and choices. As a result, HSPs are often considered inner-directed rather than outer-directed individuals. So although both HSPs and non-HSPs are social, highly sensitive people come at the social/cultural world from different natural predispositions, which have implications for their motivations, their ability to interact with others, and the possibility of being heard and seen.

1   SBU Brain Study: Sensitive Persons' Perception Moderates Responses Based On Culture, http://sb.cc.stonybrook.edu/news/general/050310SensitivePersons.php

Understanding their energy sensitivity helps HSPs get a handle on their sensitivity and challenges. To understand more about the unique highly sensitive person, let's look at Dr. Elaine Aron's "DOES" model of the highly sensitive trait.

CHAPTER 2

The 'Does' Model

Dr. Elaine Aron has created an acronym for understanding the key components of the highly sensitive nature: "DOES," a model which is a useful and accessible tool for understanding the highly sensitive trait. This chapter explores the model and includes some quotes from Dr. Aron's writing to explain the "DOES" model, which stands for:

- Depth of processing

- Overstimulation

- Emotional Reactivity

- Empathy

- Sensing the subtle

D is for Depth of Processing

Highly sensitive people have a natural kind of noticing that leads them to investigate or process deeply what they do not understand. Deep processing is a unique skill and gift, because:

- It provides highly sensitive people with a window to energetic information. Deep processing is a special kind of listening to energy that comes from one's entire being. There is no fragmentation of information. HSPs take it all in and then try to understand what the energy is telling them. The insights that result offer them the opportunity to find creative choices to many problems and situations.

- It can bring a lot of learning and awareness in spite of the fact that some energy that HSPs take in is painful and difficult.

- It brings out the best in us when we struggle with our awareness and the hard choices about what to do with our awareness.

- It helps our empathetic natures find the best in others and make choices that serve the best for all of us.

What is especially lovely about deep processing is the spirit of generosity that supports its due diligence. The innate intention to be fair behind deep processing is very respect worthy.

As Elaine Aron writes, deep processing is foundational for high sensitivity.

> "At the foundation of the trait of high sensitivity is the tendency to process information more deeply... HSPs simply process everything more, relating and comparing what they notice to their past experience with other similar things. They do it whether they are aware of it or not. When we decide without knowing how we came to that decision, we call this intuition, and HSPs have good (but not infallible!) intuition. When you make a decision consciously, you may notice that you are slower than others because you think over all the options so carefully. That's depth of processing too.

> Studies supporting the depth of processing aspect of the trait have compared the brain activation of sensitive and non-sensitive people doing various perceptual tasks. Research by Jadzia Jagiellowicz found that the highly sensitive use more of those parts of the brain associated with "deeper" processing of information, especially on tasks that involve noticing subtleties. In another study, by ourselves and others, sensitive and non-sensitive persons were given perceptual tasks that were already known to be difficult (require more brain activation or effort) depending on the culture a person is from.

The non-sensitive persons showed the usual difficulty, but the highly sensitive subjects' brains apparently did not have this difficulty, regardless of their culture. It was as if they found it natural to look beyond their cultural expectations to how things "really are."[2]

The research showing the ability of highly sensitive people to look beyond cultural expectations is important and explains why HSPs are not only more aware but also may not connect with people who align more with cultural norms. Cultural expectations around materialism and consumption are a good example of expectations that a highly sensitive person would not resonate with because of awareness of about social and environmental harms. Energy sensitivity also provides HSPs with a window into the harm experienced by sexism, racism, and other forms of discrimination. These awarenesses can create a disconnect with others.

Depth of processing is one of the most important gifts of being highly sensitive because it takes sensitive people beyond easy answers and conventional wisdom. Deep processing lets HSPs integrate people, contexts, the spoken and unspoken, the conscious and unconscious. It is rich. It can generate creative solutions, notice minute changes in someone's demeanor, and see important shifts long before they happen.

HSPs can notice when a colleague is being honest, when a family member is sad but not really showing it, and when someone is speaking in a hollow manner. Depth of processing brings color to the energy information we take in. It shows when energy is heavy, dull, fast, or whimsical. The quality of energy is the beginning of our processing and teaches us what we need to know about it.

When you take in as much information as highly sensitive people do, the first order of business is to understand what you take in. Highly sensitive people have a special way of doing that. Not only do they enter the energy to understand its qualities, but they also then try to connect

---

2   Author's Note, 2012 for The Highly Sensitive Person, 9/6/2012, http://hsperson.com/pdf/ Authors_note_HSPbk_Preface.pdf

the energetic information with their holistic, big-picture perspective. The attention of highly sensitive people travels between the energetic data and the big picture and back before action can be contemplated.

There is a benefit to highly sensitive processing. By seeking understanding before action, HSPs go beyond personal considerations to formulate an accurate understanding of what they see, hear, or feel. They may have strong feelings but their conscientiousness causes them to think before they act. As a result, a transpersonal perspective is part of their nature.

O is for Overstimulation

Noticing introduces HSPs to the fact that they are different. They notice things that others do not and take seriously things that others consider insignificant or unimportant. However, an HSP's different way of assessing their environment and a lack of validation for their perceptions can cause self-doubt and lack of confidence. The huge volume of information in their highly stimulated world can overwhelm and cause overstimulation because they become inundated by it. Deep processing and overstimulation go hand in hand. If HSPs are not careful to manage their engagement with the world, they can become exhausted and burn out.

Dr. Aron describes it as follows:

> "If you are going to notice every little thing in a situation, and if the situation is complicated (many things to remember), intense (noisy, cluttered, etc.), or goes on too long (a two-hour commute), it seems obvious that you will also have to wear out sooner from having to process so much. Others, not noticing much or any of what you have, will not tire as quickly. They may even think it quite strange that you find it too much to sightsee all day and go to a nightclub in the evening. They might talk blithely on when you need them to be quiet a moment so that you can have some time just to think, or they might enjoy an "energetic" restaurant or a party when you can hardly bear the noise. Indeed this is often the behavior we and others have noticed most—that

HSPs are easily stressed by overstimulation (including social stimulation), or having learned their lesson, that they avoid intense situations more than others do."[3]

While every historical period has had its challenges, contemporary capitalist culture presents excessive affronts to the highly sensitive person. In Western culture, speed combined with the volume of people and information has made deep processing painful for many highly sensitive people. It is unrealistic to process all of the information that HSPs take in fast enough to make sound decisions, although that is what HSPs try to do. When bombarded, a sensitive person may become indecisive to avoid making choices that are harmful. Highly sensitive people work better in slower-paced environments and cultures where people work through ideas, issues, and challenges at a more human pace. It affords them the ability to make the most constructive choices possible and provides them with the most satisfaction as a result.

An additional consideration for highly sensitive people is the impact of stressful environments. The volume of information HSPs have to process causes a lot of stress on the HSP nervous system, which when unaddressed can lead to serious health problems especially if the stress is chronic. Unsuitable work environments, which do not allow the self-pacing highly sensitive people require, can be damaging.

Overstimulation is a complex and serious issue for highly sensitive people. Because HSPs work from the inside out, which means they take in energetic information, process it deeply, and then respond from what they have learned, they can easily become depleted and stressed and burn out. Overstimulation does not just come from the volume of information a highly sensitive person needs to process but also from toxic people and environments, hyperactivity in our space, high-pressure demands, and expectations that we conform to values that are not ours. The difference

---

3   Author's Note, 2012 for The Highly Sensitive Person, 9/6/2012, http://hsperson.com/pdf/
Authors_note_HSPbk_Preface.pdf

between the highly sensitive nature and the current late-stage capitalistic culture could not be starker.

Trying to make sense of capitalistic culture, live with it, and make it work when it does not for most highly sensitive people causes many HSPs serious unhappiness and stress-related illnesses.

E is for Emotional Reactivity

Highly sensitive people respond better to positive images, according to the research by Dr. Aron cited below. Positive valence, as Dr. Aron describes it, is an important part of what it means to be highly sensitive.

Here is the research information from Dr. Aron:

> Data from surveys and experiments had already found some evidence that HSPs react more to both positive and negative experiences, but a series of studies done by Jadzia Jagiellowicz found that HSPs particularly react more than non-HSPs to pictures with a "positive valence." This was even truer if they had had a good childhood. In her studies of the brain, this reaction to positive pictures was not only in the areas associated with the initial experience of strong emotions, but also in "higher" areas of thinking and perceiving, in some of the same areas as those found in the depth-of-processing brain studies. This stronger reaction to positive pictures being even more enhanced by a good childhood fits with a new concept suggested by Michael Pluess and Jay Belsky, the idea of "vantage sensitivity," which they created in order to highlight the specific potential for sensitive people to benefit from positive circumstances and interventions.[4]

Highly sensitive people will express the need to live and work in positive and constructive environments, which have humanistic values, respect people (including their employees), and serve a positive purpose in the

---

4   Author's Note, 2012 for The Highly Sensitive Person, 9/6/2012, http://hsperson.com/pdf/ Authors_note_HSPbk_Preface.pdf

world. HSPs require a supportive management structure with low infighting and negative internal politics and the ability to pace themselves so that they can work effectively. Incessant negativity is wearing and just another form of stress that exhausts them. Negativity surfaces where problems stay unresolved, which is not positive for anyone, especially highly sensitive people. Because of their positive valence, HSPs will stick with a problem until it is resolved, which makes negative environments where problems do not get resolved a burden.

Highly sensitive people need to be in a positive place in their relationships and work. It is a natural need that does not stem from ego but from the need to be at peace with themselves. A "positive valence," which is a response to positive imagery, causes HSPs to seek positive situations for work and relationships. It can be characterized as a "constructive spirit" which is generosity at work and for a highly sensitive person a path to inner peace. HSPs have a predisposition to be constructive and need the opportunity to do so to be happy.

Trust is an important topic for many highly sensitive people who report they have difficulty finding a way to be trusted by others. Since HSPs are different temperamentally and physically, and have humanistic values that are at odds with the cultural objectives of the Western world, they are uncomfortable and others are uncomfortable with them. There are many people with whom highly sensitive people will not have a close relationship for the reasons just cited. Although it is not a preference, HSPs have to expect that some relationships will be only transitory and transactional.

People with whom HSPs share values are those who are most likely to trust highly sensitive people. Although other people many not understand and trust them, it is important to realize that the positive valence Dr. Aron refers to is a kind of insurance that our natural predisposition is constructive.

E Is Also For Empathy

Empathy is one of the most important characteristics of highly sensitive people. One definition of empathy from the Merriam-Webster dictionary that suits highly sensitive people is:

> the action of understanding, being aware of, being sensitive to, and vicariously experiencing the feelings, thoughts, and experience of another of either the past or present without having the feelings, thoughts, and experience fully communicated in an objectively explicit manner. [5]

As the definition states, empathy is an action of understanding. Therefore, empathy is a valuable research tool and not just a way to connect with others. It allows you to investigate energetic differences and learn more about them. Dr. Aron confirms the wisdom-serving basis of empathy in her research:

> In another study, by Bianca Acevedo, sensitive and non-sensitive persons looked at photos of both strangers and loved ones expressing happiness, sadness, or a neutral feeling. In all situations, when there was emotion in the photo, sensitive persons showed increased activation in the insula, but also more activity in their mirror neuron system, especially when looking at the happy faces of loved ones... Not only do these amazing neurons help us learn through imitation, but in conjunction with the other areas of the brain that were especially active for HSPs, they help us know others' intentions and how they feel. Hence they are largely responsible for the universal human capacity for empathy. We do not just know how someone else feels, but actually feel that way ourselves to some extent. This is very familiar to sensitive people. Anyone's sad faces tended to generate more activity in these mirror neurons in HSPs than others. When seeing photos of their loved ones being unhappy, sensitive persons also showed more activation in areas suggesting they wanted to do something, to act, even more than in areas involving empathy (perhaps we learn to cool

---

5   Merriam-Webster, http://www.merriam-webster.com/dictionary/empathy

down our intense empathy in order to help). But overall, brain activation indicating empathy was stronger in HSPs than non-HSPs when looking at photos of faces showing strong emotion of any type. [6]

Emotions are windows to energetic information. When emotions are combined with the positive valence that motivates HSPs it is easy to see why highly sensitive people are empathetic and how they can become people pleasers, putting the needs of others before their own.

When highly sensitive people take in energy, they are taking in all the energy around them including the energy of others. Think of it as holding a large ball of energy in your hand with all of the energy from everyone around you. You will understandably be curious about what all the energy is telling you. In a world as hyper-stimulated as Western culture, it is inevitable that addressing the huge amount of energy you take in will result in displacing your own needs and feelings.

As a result, HSPs can engage in the people-pleasing behaviors of not expressing their own needs, not rocking the boat, and finding it difficult to say no. There are some natural reasons for doing this:

- The highly sensitive person does not have enough time to process all the energy they take in. In this circumstance, a highly sensitive person may choose to support another rather than cause potential harm, so what is perceived as people pleasing is really conscientiousness on the part of the sensitive person.

- The highly sensitive person may be unable to separate their energy from the energy of another person— it takes time to discern whose energy is whose—so they may become over responsible for the feelings, needs, and desires of others. Deep

---

6   Author's Note, 2012 for The Highly Sensitive Person, 9/6/2012, http://hsperson.com/pdf/ Authors_note_HSPbk_Preface.pdf

down, however, HSPs want to see everyone happy because of their natural altruism.

Empathy offers many gifts. It is a good strategic tool because it lets you see into the heart of someone or even something. It lets you see the dreams and limits in a situation so that you can make intelligent decisions and find constructive actions.

Empathy provides you with a window into the heart so that you can see compatibility between people, situations, agendas, and plans. It also helps you be in touch with the processes in your environment. You can notice when the process is rushed or stagnant. The energy HSPs notice can inform their intuition so that their intuition can give them a red or green light on an action, strategy, or plan.

S Is For Sensing The Subtle

Sensitivity to nuance and subtleties is the innate capacity HSPs have for connecting to everything in our world. In this reference, Dr. Aron discusses this characteristic further:

> Most of the studies already cited required perceiving sub-
> tleties. This is often what is most noticeable to us person-
> ally, the little things we notice that others miss. Given that,
> and because I called the trait high sensitivity, many have
> thought this is the heart of the trait. (To correct this confusion
> and emphasize the role of processing, we used "sensory
> processing sensitivity" as its more formal, scientific designa-
> tion.) However, this trait is not so much about extraordinary
> senses— after all, there are sensitive people who have poor
> eyesight or hearing. True, some sensitive people report that
> one or more senses are very acute, but even in these cases
> it could be that they process the sensory information more
> carefully rather than having something unusual about their
> eyes, nose, skin, taste buds, or ears. Again, the brain areas
> that are more active when sensitive people perceive are
> those that do the more complex processing of sensory infor-
> mation. Not so much the areas that recognize alphabet

letters by their shape or even that read words, but the areas that catch the subtle meaning of words.

Our awareness of subtleties is useful in an infinite number of ways, from simple pleasure in life to strategizing our response based on our awareness of others' nonverbal cues (that they may have no idea they are giving off) about their mood or trustworthiness. Of course, on the other hand, when we are worn out we may be the least aware of anything, subtle or gross, except our own need for a break. [7]

Subtleties are clues to what is going on. They tell you the minute changes in someone or some situation, signaling when appearances are deceiving or something is changing. Nuances provide you with insights and are windows into the depths of what you are working on or to which you are paying attention. Subtleties make it easier to let go of judgments so that you can develop a more informed opinion.

Subtleties are what many highly sensitive people draw on that create the perception of genius. It lets them see possibilities that others miss, connect the dots in a new way, and express a fuller perspective. Subtleties humanize you by enlarging your perspective beyond superficialities and stereotypes; they locate the good in others, especially those who are different. A perfect example is the comedic genius of Robin Williams, who used his sensitivity and insight to help us all see the world in new ways.

Subtleties also support creativity by offering you possibilities you may not have considered, creative paths that are fresh and unlikely connections to add a new wrinkle to what is known.

(To read more from the article on Dr. Aron's site, visit http://hsperson. com/pdf/Authors_note_HSPbk_Preface.pdf)

---

7   Author's Note, 2012 for The Highly Sensitive Person, 9/6/2012, http://hsperson.com/pdf/ Authors_note_HSPbk_Preface.pdf

Why Sensitivity Is Important

Sensitivity gives you the ability to connect with all creatures and beings in your environment. You can listen to the world from your inner being and connect beyond the spoken word. You can see the real being in others, human and animal. You hear with your nervous systems what is said and unsaid.

The highly sensitive trait is a gift for energetic intelligence. The fundamental orientation of HSPs is energetic, which means that they listen to what energy tells them and then form their goals. Non-HSPs form their goals differently—perhaps based on more external factors like tradition, cultural values, goals, and incentives.

Looking at individual characteristics of the sensitive person is helpful. However, the real magic of sensitivity comes from the combination of the characteristics:

- The HSP's sponge-like nervous systems make them present, which sometimes feels awful in a world that seems to be stuck in the past or focused on the future. It is one of the reasons HSPs can feel so alone. Being alone with the world's energy gives them a window on the magnificence of life, which puts them in touch with awe and therefore gratitude. It lets them invite others into a new world beyond the mundane and seek new solutions. It brings out their creativity.

- Being present means being present to everything, which is like having a live thermometer as part of your nervous system. HSPs feel the immediacy of the pain, joy, yearning, and unmet needs in others and themselves. When you feel so much, you become tender to life in all its forms. It brings out your conscientiousness and desire to make life better.

- Being present with their energetic intelligence gives HSPs a level of intimacy with the world that puts them in a different place, often creating distance with others and loneliness for themselves. It lets them observe subtle distinctions about other people which, when revealed, can cause others to feel understood or uncomfortable and exposed.

- Since HSPs experience the entire disharmony in the world, harmony is what they naturally seek and what informs many of their choices. The drive for harmony is behind their conscientiousness.

- Gentleness is a precursor to delight because to be gentle is to be open to wonder. Wonder leads to questions, which leads to new ideas and creative solutions.

- The desire to put a smile on someone's face is an important motivator for sensitive people with a "positive valence." When you take in all of the world's energy, the only direction possible is a constructive one because you cannot knowingly contribute to the world's pain.

- Being present to all energy means that you search for the sweet spot in meeting the moment: the right solution, the best choice, because your nervous systems tell you how important it is.

- Being present and conscientious activates your creativity so that you can find the best solutions in any situation.

Each of the characteristics of the "DOES" model provides highly sensitive people with an important talent for energy sensitivity, and HSPs may be pioneers in the development of more sophisticated human intelligence through their sensitivity. Being energy sensitive lets you see beyond the many narratives about social roles and social identity as well as the "shoulds" and "oughts" that occupy our social space, as Dr. Aron says. This ability lets you develop a big-picture perspective that can be useful and freeing. It lets you see beyond created differences of sex, race, and religion to a larger transpersonal and inclusive view of others. It lets you see yourself in others.

A Gift For Balance And Complexity

The energy sensitivity of highly sensitive people attunes them to the enormity of the possibility in the universe. They notice when all aspects of life are aligned and when they are misaligned. They notice when their energy levels are unable to handle the demands of others. They notice when demands being made do not take into account time and resource constraints. They notice excesses and their consequences.

These gifts are not always appreciated by a world that often prefers various forms of simplification. Highly sensitive people are often considered slow when they are better thought of as thorough. Speed and sensitivity are incompatible. Being labeled slow causes highly sensitive people to become defensive about themselves and sometime to try to fit into the high-speed world. As a result, highly sensitive people often find it difficult to bring their gifts to the world in a way that satisfies their gentle, empathetic natures.

Highly sensitive people can help the world find greater congruence between all the different forces at play in the world: the needs of humans, the requirements of animals and the environment, and the competing needs of social groups. Our sensitivity seeks fairness, which is a wonderful gift to give to the world.

How can you create a great life for yourself and bring your gifts into the world? To get started, let's get some perspective on where you are and your possible role in this evolving world.

What's Missing That HSPs Need

Highly sensitive people are aware, compassionate, and holistic so they are naturally inclusive in how they approach life and problems. However,

HSPs flounder when they do not know what to do with all the information they take in.

This chart points to what is missing for HSPs.

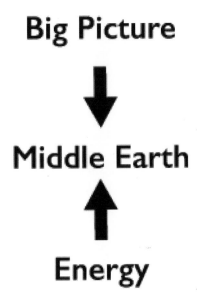

Big Picture

Middle Earth

Energy

Highly sensitive people excel at energy awareness and the big picture: the top and bottom of the chart. Energy awareness is all the raw materials HSPs take in, some of which they do not know what to do with. Big-picture skills develop from the raw material of energy as HSPs try to make sense of the information they process. Highly sensitive people go back and forth between the energy data they take in and the big picture to make sense of the world and what they are experiencing.

The empathetic nature of highly sensitive people causes them to construct a humanistic, inclusive approach to life because their nervous systems do not really exclude information. Their nerves are equal opportunity nerves!

"Middle Earth," the place of our daily lives, is about manifestation, which is where HSPs struggle because they are not tactically oriented. HSPs are energetically, holistically, and service oriented, which gives them more of a long-term focus. However, since they take in everything, a highly sensitive person will notice tactics—any actions taken by others to accomplish an objective—but they notice the energy around those tactics even more. Because HSPs have a positive valence, as Elaine Aron's research shows, they notice when tactics are harmful or aggressive but they do not necessarily know how to respond, especially since many highly sensitive people associate tactics with aggression.

Highly sensitive people are known for being compassionate and humanitarian, although not saints! They seek to engage in a way that creates positive and constructive outcomes so sometimes they cannot find the right approach to create the result they want. When that happens, HSPs can become indecisive and think less of themselves.

To put their awareness to use, HSPs need frameworks that enable them to process energy information effectively so that they can find ways to interact with others more effectively and make choices that they are proud of and that are effective in "Middle Earth."

We will be discussing frameworks in the next section.

SECTION 2: THE IMPORTANCE AND VALUE OF FRAMEWORKS

Overview

Section 2 is a journey into one of the most valuable tools for navigating the world: frameworks. You will discover what frameworks are, the different types of frameworks, and why they are important. Then you will explore the evolutional framework of Spiral Dynamics, which helps you make sense of how the world works. Finally, you will learn why frameworks are so important for HSPs and how they can be used successfully.

CHAPTER 3

The Importance And Value Of Frameworks

Frameworks are great tools for helping you navigate the world.

People have many ways of handling the uncertainty of life. Some have a set of beliefs or ideologies. Others have a role that anchors them. Still others have a religion or purpose. All of these can be helpful, but they are not always flexible in a constantly changing world.

To be as effective as possible in life, it is useful to have frameworks. Frameworks help us in a variety of situations. The wonderful thing about frameworks is that they help us deal with something but are never the thing itself. They are a concept, an outline, or a skeleton. Once a framework is in place, roles, beliefs and ideologies follow to create the social structure that supports the framework. A tribal culture is a different framework than an entrepreneurial culture like capitalism. Each has its own beliefs, ideologies, and roles or divisions of labor. So there is an overarching framework that is like a worldview that then creates subframeworks around beliefs and roles.

When building a house, you create a framework from architectural drawings and then add the building parts onto it to complete the structure.

Each building is custom and personal to a degree. If you look at ranch houses or cottages, you will notice many similarities and unique features. Some will share a basic shape but climate differences may dictate different building materials. Buildings will share structural elements like kitchens but will also offer many stylistic variables.

Frameworks evolve over time. A simple ranch structure may be satisfactory at one point in time and later a framework for additions may be needed and created.

Human beings are a great example of frameworks in action. Our skeletons are our physical framework, and look at all of the differences between us. Some are tall or short, thin or stocky, and we all have many skin colors, talents, and interests. The variety in humans is huge. The human framework has evolved from the frameworks of simpler creatures as nature has become more complex.

Subframeworks are part of a larger framework. These subframeworks around social, cultural, and economic functions are like the building blocks of the cultural system and allow for greater complexity and functionality in the system. They help create common ground with others so that people can work together as part of a larger cultural system that defines the purpose of the culture. Each of these subframeworks identify "correct" values, behaviors, and standards for everyone to follow.

Frameworks are tools for building and relating. Whether you are building relationships, careers, houses, communities, a strong body, or a daily schedule that lets live in a healthy way, frameworks are what you can use to make it easier for yourself to make decisions and choices so that you can have more of what you want and need in life.

CHAPTER 4

What Is A Framework?

What is a framework? We have already described it and what it does. Let's go a little deeper.

According to the Merriam-Webster dictionary, a framework is:

- the basic structure of something : a set of ideas or facts that provide support for something.

- a supporting structure : a structural frame.

- a basic supporting part or structure: the framework of an argument. [8]

Frameworks apply to everything, and they always have a purpose. When you begin to understand the framework for something, you can understand its purpose and can then relate intelligently and with intention.

Frameworks apply to cultures, constitutions, gender relations, organizational structure, how we structure our day, natural cycles, all natural organisms, and all growth and development. You cannot escape frameworks.

Frameworks can make life easier or more difficult. Once a framework has been established, it can be difficult to change. People become attached to their frameworks because they become an anchor in their lives. A lot of identity issues are problems related to unsuitable or inappropriate frameworks.

Frameworks are an important building block of culture. Institutions, organizations, governments, rules, and roles are all built around frameworks.

8   Merriam-Webster, http://www.merriam-webster.com/dictionary/framework

If the frameworks support healthy human living, all is well. If they do not, the frameworks become a burden to the people living in the culture. Frameworks are created to respond to life conditions and, like all things, need to adapt to changing conditions. When they do not because of resistance to change, people and the culture are hurt by the refusal to adapt to changing conditions. A great example is the failure to adapt governmental and industry behaviors to accommodate the realities of climate change.

Although frameworks are fixed, they are not absolute and they are not immortal. They are meant to support specific objectives for a specific period of time. Some frameworks, especially cultural ones, become fixed because the creation, implementation, and support of them require substantial investments and transcend generations. So people start to think of them as "reality" when they are simply the framework-du-jour.

When countries go to war, they are often not going to war against each other. They are often going to war against each other's frameworks. Recent wars such as the Iraq War between the United States and Iraq are, among other things, wars between different frameworks: the entrepreneurial frameworks of Western culture and the frameworks of tribal and religious cultures. Frameworks can be personal but generally they have a larger social membership, which is one reason change is difficult. It takes a critical mass of people to change their minds so that a framework can change.

Frameworks are our conditioning and what so many of us try to release in order to live better lives. Some of the pain that HSPs pick up in the world is the pain of unhappy conditioned people and the unhappiness of people living in frameworks that are unsuitable.

Frameworks and conditioning are not all mental. For thousands of years, the accepted theory was that the mind and body functioned separately. That theory is incorrect. The research of neuroscientist Candace

Pert found a biological connection with our minds, what we now call the mind-body connection.[9] The mind-body connection demonstrates that conditioning is not just mental, it is biological as well, and the connection shows us that the subconscious mind is located in the body.

Our thoughts and feelings create peptides that flood our bodies. Over time, our cells develop receptors for those peptides, which means that the receptors actively seek more of what they have been getting. There are peptides and receptors for each feeling and thought. This is important because we often think by changing our thoughts we change our reality, and that is true up to a point. Most people do not realize that their perceptual framework is also located in their bodies, which is why so many people try to change and fail. They do not realize that it takes a sustained effort to change the peptide receptors in the body to create the change they desire. As a result, they have a feeling of failure around change.

The frameworks of culture have been coded into our entire body's cells, not just our minds, through repetition. Frameworks are concepts hardwired into us through the conditioning we receive as children. It takes a considerable effort redirecting our thoughts, behaviors, and biology to release social and cultural conditioning.

Our institutions and cultures are also intellectually wired to a framework as all of us are biologically. This may sound depressing and would be if the world were fixed, which it is not. In fact, in spite of efforts to control the world and keep it fixed and stable, in reality it is always changing, albeit slowly.

When highly sensitive people take in all of the energy around them, they are taking in, among other things, the dissonance of different frameworks bumping into each other and the challenges of people trying to work in a world of many frameworks. Some of the pain in the world comes from frameworks that are too rigid or inappropriate for a situation:

---

9   The Research of Candace Pert, PhD, http://www.healingcancer.info/ebook/candace-pert

1. Rigid frameworks around sex roles cause pain all around and prevents the full realization of all human potential.

2. Religious frameworks that do not acknowledge climate change prevent timely solutions to a growing catastrophic situation.

3. Tribal frameworks are unable to access skills and tools of modern society and modern cultures are not able to respect the knowledge and wisdom about nature that tribal systems offer.

Some highly sensitive people, because of their natural energetic connection especially with nature may feel that they live outside of the current dominant framework, the entrepreneurial capitalistic system of the Western world, and that is true for many HSPs. That difference alone accounts for much of the loneliness that HSPs feel, and it is one of the reasons HSPs struggle with connection.

It is very difficult to be the lone person marching to a different drummer—something that highly sensitive people know a lot about. However, frameworks also offer HSPs the potential to remain true to themselves while relating to people operating from the rich variety of frameworks in the world. Frameworks are not necessarily unhealthy, and they can be extremely valuable.

The best frameworks recognize the need to adapt to change. Even if cultures avoid change, they cannot postpone or eliminate it by ignoring failures in the culture. Unfortunately though, people become very attached to their frameworks and sometimes lose perspective about them.

We will now look at the history through the eyes of the evolution framework of Spiral Dynamics to get perspective on how major cultural frameworks have changed over time.

CHAPTER 5

Evolution As A Framework

The past fifty years have brought significant progress in identifying patterns so that we can understand how the world works better. Some have been generated through computing and others through research projects.

One research project conducted by Dr. Clare Graves at Utica College in New York discovered the patterns of human and cultural evolution. It is called Spiral Dynamics. It was introduced to the world by the two authors who wrote the book, Spiral Dynamics, about this amazing framework: Don Beck and Chris Cowan. Spiral Dynamics maps the stages of cultural evolution, which also happen to mirror the stages of development in individuals.

Spiral Dynamics maps the stages of evolution; people and cultures can exist at any stage, although at any given point in time one is dominant. The entrepreneurial culture of capitalism is dominant at this time. Just because the dominant culture is at one stage does not mean that everyone in that society is at that stage as well. Some people may live at prior stages of evolution; they are custodians of ancient knowledge and skills. At each cultural stage there are also people looking to the future who are already working on the next stages to come. We sometimes call them pathfinders. Anyone can be a pathfinder, but most people align with their cultural norms and remain there throughout their lives. There is nothing intrinsically wrong with being at a different stage of development or being a part of your current cultural system. Each has its benefit and contribution. It is only when a stage of development becomes toxic, abusive in some way, that it is problematic.

The chart below shows the evolutional framework of humans and cultures. The chart categories are: the name/description of the cultural structure, when it emerged, its purpose or agenda, skills it develops, and where people at that stage find joy. Each evolutional stage or framework is the primary framework for society at one point in time. Each stage is created to solve a problem and helps us to develop new skills to solve the problem it is addressing. Once we learn one set of skills, we are able to build on them to create new ways of living. Just as a child crawls, walks and then runs, so human cultures have started with baby steps and evolved to the high-speed culture we have today.

Each stage has a period of emergence, maturity, and an ending phase when a new framework emerges. Every stage emerges because of a real life necessity, creates order out of chaos, and then become the source of chaos when living conditions change. Each creates a full cultural system including beliefs, purpose, joys, punishments, institutions, and heroes held up as models for everyone else. Most people treat their stage of development as "the answer," and it is for a time until it becomes apparent that there is something new to learn. Then the process of creating a new stage of development begins. It is a never-ending cycle.

These are the stages:

Type	When Emerged	Objective	Skills	Joy
Clan	100,000 years ago	Survival	hunting, gathering	getting through the day
Tribe	50,000 years ago	mystical connection with nature, ancestors	Farming, group connection through rituals, family	appeasing spirits
Empire	10,000 years ago	conquest, discovery	fighting, exploring, engineering	winning
Authoritarian	5,000 years ago	monotheism, self sacrifice	deferred gratification, bureaucracy	order
Entrepreneurial	1,000 years ago	materialism, achievement	complex organizations, multitasking	achievement
Egalitarian	150 years ago	humanism, sharing, inclusion	sharing, healing, restoring the Earth	inclusion
Integrative	50 years ago	integration of complex systems	systems integration	making the world work
Holistic	30 years ago	holistic living, gaia consciousness	holistic, integrative thinking	living simply and mindfully

The human race started with loose bands and clans of hunter-gatherers. With the invention of agriculture, a tribal system was developed—a more permanent and less nomadic cultural system that believed in mystical spirits and connections with the ancestors. They developed elaborate rituals including sacrifice to appease the gods and ancestors. It was the first human communal system.

When the tribal system became too stifling or was unable to support its members, some struck out on their own. They formed warrior groups like the Vikings plundering villages and taking whatever they wanted. These warrior groups conquered as many people as they could, creating huge empires. The last were the Romans. This was the first individualistic stage of development and has been compared to the terrible twos. It is seen today in gangs.

When the empire system was out of control, a new system started to develop. It was a monotheistic system, which created an afterlife and purpose for its members in serving the church. The fear of god was the one thing that could control out-of-control empire warriors, and this authoritarian system brought some much-needed order to the world. Religions created economies around their churches and monasteries. They put people to work serving the church and developed administrative skills and bureaucracies. Everyone had a place and was expected to stay in it. This is the second communal stage of human development.

Many found the religious authoritarian system oppressive, especially the scientists who were developing new theories about how the world worked through their experiments. They were the pathfinders seeking a way to improve the material comfort of life and help people live longer and better lives.

At the time, there was a lot of experimentation going on under the radar because the church did not approve of scientific investigations. Science was being used to create all sorts of new tools. Some people developed machines to create new modes of transportation and to produce much-needed goods for improved quality of life. Others were using science to find medicines to treat the many illnesses that shortened people's lives. They developed and commercialized many improvements like indoor plumbing. In some ways, the beginning of the material age was a godsend for people whose material comforts were negligible. This stage was the second evolutional stage where the focus and the cultural structure were individualistic. Achievement, gaining status through accomplishment, and claiming material wealth were all goals of this stage. This is the current global system and is in the process of changing into the next communal stage, which the chart shows started one hundred fifty years ago.

With material wealth comes an opportunity to share that wealth. The next communal stage will deal with the excesses of materialism while leveling the playing field and creating a culture of inclusion. It will be a time of healing the wounds of division. This new stage started in the last century. Movements for fairness, environmental sustainability, and individual efforts at healing the pain of the past have been underway for some time. The egalitarian system that is developing will address sustainability issues which are a global emergency, while protecting shared natural and cultural resources.

After the healing work of the egalitarian age, the human race will be moving on to more advanced stages which will seek to reduce fragmentation and the problems created by division by integrating all the systems of the past into a workable whole. The world will also be seeking greater peace through holistic, sustainable living that supports quality of life around the globe. The human race has come far, made a lot of mistakes and is now starting a cleanup process that will hopefully put us on a more secure footing. Up until now, the agenda of humanity has been survival. Now that survival has been achieved, we need to turn our attention to peace and quality of life.

As mentioned earlier, these stages of development play out in the individual as well as the culture. People who are at the same stage as a culture feel right at home. Those who are in a different place usually do not.

Each of these stages creates a cultural structure. The empire level was a time of discovery and conquest, which created large empires like the Roman Empire. Each stage also defines the "right person" and way of being for that stage of development. The authoritarian level best found in the major religious systems expects obedience to a higher authority, self-sacrifice, and each person knowing and staying in their place.

Each cultural stage begins in response to some life conditions that forces change, usually created by the excesses of the prior system. We are currently evolving from the materialistic/entrepreneurial level to a humanistic level that will emphasize sustainability and inclusion. This change is occurring because materialism combined with population size is not a sustainable framework any longer and because more people are self-governing and therefore expect to have a say in their own lives.

So necessity drives change and the creation of cultural systems, which defines values, rules, and expectations. Each stage creates a cultural story that is acted out in everyday life and that serves to bond the group members. Aboriginal Dreamtime is one example; the American Dream is another. Everyone is expected to conform to the rules, roles and the story agenda and is rewarded for doing so.

The creation of cultural systems is a human pattern that has been going on for centuries, although we are only becoming aware of this pattern now. In the past, people have not handled the evolution of one system to another with grace. People who are at different stages of development are often rejected, which is unnecessary and counterproductive. Each of these stages of development can be healthy or unhealthy depending on how it is developed. Each has something to give to us and skills that it develops that we need. When we reject any stage, we are rejecting a part of ourselves; it is much better to seek the healthy manifestation of a level than to reject it.

Before moving on to how HSPs can use frameworks, note in the chart above that the current entrepreneurial system began 1,000 years ago and is aging. The next cultural framework, egalitarian, is one hundred fifty years old, so it has not yet come into its own; however it is the new system that people refer to when they talk about the Great Turning. Systemic change takes a long time.

CHAPTER 6

The Use Of Frameworks For HSPs

Highly sensitive people can benefit from using frameworks that let them process what they take in more effectively. It can almost become an energy protection shield that you consult before making decisions and taking action. Frameworks can let you see into the heart and intent of others through a different lens so that you do not respond to others from your wounds, which tend to make relationships more difficult.

Frameworks give you a context to work from with others that takes you out of a personal dynamic to a transpersonal one so you can seek a constructive outcome for the situation involved. When you suspend your desires or expectations, you can formulate goals that are appropriate and have some chance of a positive outcome.

Frameworks give you a chance for success on the world's terms without sacrificing your interest in positive outcomes and without sacrificing the positive valence that Dr. Aron has discovered in HSPs. They leave your integrity intact while offering you ways to know what to let go of and what is not yours. They help you activate your creativity to solve problems while not assuming responsibility for others.

We will discuss frameworks more in the next section as we discuss the challenge that highly sensitive people have had fitting into the current system and how the new emerging framework offers new possibilities for highly sensitive people.

SECTION 3: GETTING A HANDLE ON THE WORLD

Overview

The third section explores more deeply the current dominant world economic and cultural system and how it affects highly sensitive people, the role of highly sensitive people in it, and how changing trends and important shifts are creating new opportunities for HSPs to create a fulfilling life.

CHAPTER 7

Why HSPs Have Been Marginalized

We live in a fear-based world. We see this today in the competitive rush to make money and the difficulty people have accepting others who are different whether because of race, sexual orientation, or culture. Fear dominated most early human societies, and we have carried that fear forward to a large degree. Fear is problematic for many reasons. For highly sensitive people, the energy of fear is not only exhausting but also tends to create more problems than it solves because it adds to and muddies the other energies they take in.

The fear-based world of capitalism has a driven energy and is time sensitive. Its demands for speed compress the time available for energy processing, which does not resonate well with the gentle listening qualities of highly sensitive energy. HSPs have difficulty processing energy in a timely way to respond to demands of this fast-paced system because of their deep processing needs as discussed earlier in the "DOES" model.

Highly sensitive people have been cultural outsiders for a long time. Although studies show that the sensitive trait exists in over 100 species[10] as well as humans now known as highly sensitive people, this unique type of human has not been recognized especially since they do not sync with

10 Evolutionary emergence of responsive and unresponsive personalities, Proceedings Of The National Academy Of Sciences Of The United States Of America, http://www.pnas.org/content/105/41/15825.full, June, 2008

the drives of fear-based cultures. That seems to be especially true in the high-speed automated world of today.

Early humans had the need for sensitive trackers and healers with herbal and shamanic skills, talents that highly sensitive people could offer to serve their tribes and social groups. Automated tools now provide surveillance for security and mechanized tools for high-tech medicine. Capitalism has devalued the gentle soul who notices changes in flora or animal tracks. A medical system that micromanages symptoms but leave diseases to fester disdains the intuitive healer of the past who listens to and treats negative energies.

In addition, the human race in its vulnerability has invested its attention and resources to support military power, which has now mushroomed into trillion dollar mountains of destructive capability although the cost of war in damaged lives and environment seems to be creating more street and online protests. The survival-driven human race has lost sight of its connection to nature and its need to be in nature. Humans think they dominate nature and manipulate it to serve their desires and mitigate their fears. Fear may be big business, but highly sensitive people know how misguided it can be as a basis for human society.

Innumerable environmental crises are offering us a wakeup call while losing the competition for our attention to media noise, entertainment, and the daily rush of humans trying to make life work on a competitive and overcrowded planet. HSPs can get lost in the shuffle.

The Early Fear Of Being Labeled Defective

Early human tribes and cultures had few resources to sustain life. People rarely lived long due to disease, or the threat of animals and weather conditions, which overwhelmed their self-protective resources. So survival meant conserving resources to serve those who best supported the survival of the group. The aggressive and strong came first. Those who were not needed or were handicapped in some way had difficulty surviving. Being labeled defective could be a death sentence.

The fear of being labeled defective did not stop at physical attributes. Early cultures punished those considered responsible for unfortunate events including crop failures and other problems. Human sacrifice appeased the gods and a highly sensitive person could become a target if they did not offer tracking, shamanic or other skills that the group valued. Early cultures also had extreme competitions, which meant death to the loser, so highly sensitive people who were probably not as physically gifted as warriors could be vulnerable.

War cultures value brawn, aggression, and fighting skills, which are not part of the highly sensitive tool kit. From the early days of human life, highly sensitive people have been vulnerable because they are different and they carry a fear for their safety to this day. HSP fears are valid because humans have targeted those who are different for centuries. At this time, a crossroad in human living and identity, HSPs can afford to not only accept their fears but also to reconsider them. Being different is now out in the open as more as more people assert their right to be who they are. Highly sensitive people have as much a right to do so as anyone else.

Although many sensitives may want to continue to keep their heads down because some people still disrespect sensitivity, highly sensitive people can protect themselves from those who are contemptuous of sensitivity while challenging their own ideas about what is possible for themselves. We will be discussing new opportunities later.

Modern Defectiveness

Cultures have always labeled some people defective and discriminated against them: The Untouchables in India and the witches of the Middle Ages are just two examples. Ethnic and racial "defectiveness" is as common as the labeling of unwanted personality characteristics.

Once ideas about acceptability and defectiveness are established and accepted by the culture at large, scapegoating is inevitable for those who are labeled as defective. So those who are unwelcome have to forge a separate path for themselves. In current cultures dominated by complex economic systems and many natural resources controlled by private interests, opting out of the "system" is difficult, which means survival can be challenging for HSPs. Many highly sensitive people hide their sensitivity in order to survive, which can destroy their health, or try to find employment that will accommodate their nature even if it is not the work they would like. As a result, highly sensitive people often live with a lot of discomfort because of unwanted compromises and the belief that life cannot be what they would like it to be.

Conformity And The Loss Of Self

One reason that many highly sensitive people struggle to make a life for themselves is that their natural goodness is not the goodness that is valued and rewarded by our current cultural system. Being an outsider does not make an HSP undeserving—highly sensitive people are abundantly talented. But when your culture values something different, it is as if the people around you have blinders on and they cannot see you; if they do, they may be uncomfortable with your different nature.

Whether because you are in touch with your true self and feel you have to hide or because you are not aware of your true self from trying to belong, when you conform to survive you will experience a loss of self. Conforming means you lose the ability to participate in constructing an agenda that lets you serve from your important gifts of empathy, insight, and creativity. In conforming, you are expected to live by the fast-paced production values of your culture that do not suit your sensitive nature and cause you to feel less competent, when in reality HSPs are just differently competent.

Conformity creates a lot of loss. If people are simply consumers and that is their value, what about all of their natural talents and gifts that have nothing to do with the economic system? If something cannot be consumed, is it important and valuable? Many people have come to define their value in the context of the economic system, which means that the economic system defines them. Although highly sensitive people tend not to be defined by their economic system, they nonetheless can feel judged as "less than" by others. Even if they know the judgments are wrong, they can hurt nonetheless.

The Framework Of Capitalism

Capitalism is a specific cultural framework, as discussed in the frameworks section. It locates power in the individual rather than the group and supports private over public interests. It sees an individual as an island unto himself/herself and devalues social supports because they take away resources than can be used for capitalistic objectives. Being a progress-oriented framework, capitalism invests in science and technology because it reveres the mind and rationality. The "mind over matter" idea of how the world works and the dualistic belief systems are part of the capitalistic framework. It could not be more unnatural, especially for the highly sensitive person.

Capitalism relies on the invention and proliferation of machines. The human body is a machine, politics is a machine, and the economy is essentially a machine for profits. Machines have no heart and soul, they do not need rest, and their parts can be replaced. They have almost become more important than people. Many people, both sensitives and non-sensitives, struggle with the demands of a system built around machines that never sleep. It makes being human a disadvantage.

The cultural energy of capitalism is the energy of machines. Even the arts use terms like "artistic production." The energy of capitalism has a uniform, repetitive, and driven beat. In contrast the energy of nature is flowing and more wavelike. When you are conditioned to your culture, you are conditioned to the energy of it. If the energy is warlike, you internalized that energy. If it is mechanistic, you internalize that energy.

When you understand that your body creates peptide receptors for the internalized patterns and values of the culture, you can understand how many people who do not realize that their energy body is tied to the mechanized energy of capitalism feel lost when away from it. People who are out in nature when they do not have an experience or connection with nature often feel bored. For highly sensitive people, nature is their natural energetic connection, not the cultural energy.

Machines perform; performance is what matters. Production is an important objective in capitalism and was essential in the early stage. However, in late-stage capitalism, where many basic needs have been met, the economy invents needs to keep factories busy and profits flowing. The system needs what it needs to stay alive. This is where it gets interesting because you would think that with all the mechanized output available, you would be swimming in high quality of life. But that is not the case.

The original intent of capitalism was to improve quality of life by mass-producing goods to serve the unmet needs of people who lived predominantly on farms barely surviving.[11] Many died young due to disease, since little was understood about the causes of illness. Mass production spread the cost of manufacturing over thousands if not millions of products, which brought down prices and made many products more accessible. Most people did not have adequate housing, indoor plumbing, or even enough food. Capitalism has made life much more comfortable and solved many problems.

In late-stage capitalism, the system seeks to generate the greatest revenue for the least cost to reward shareholders. Businesses are judged, rewarded, and punished based on their ability to show improvements in revenue and profit growth. Growth is capitalism's objective. Limits to growth are not tolerated.

---

11 Preindustrial Society, bcp.org, http://webs.bcp.org/sites/vcleary/ModernWorldHistoryTextbook/IndustrialRevolution/PreIndus.html

Many products that businesses now create are no longer necessities, so it takes a lot of effort to create demand and market products to generate the sales needed to sustain a capitalistic enterprise. These additional marketing costs, as well as the competitive nature of financial markets, drive up costs, and as a result something has to be sacrificed in the interests of financial performance. To obtain quantities of sales, product quality often suffers.

Many products do not serve the common good any longer because the resources required to produce them when they have a short life cycle places a burden on landfills and the pocketbooks of consumers. Capitalism, which avoids or eliminates costs in order to achieve financial objectives, transfers the avoided costs to others, especially government and the individual—infrastructure that support business and health care costs are good examples of this. The burden of cost transfer has been building to the point where individuals and the environment can no longer sustain them.

Highly sensitive people do not tolerate well the heavy burdens of capitalism. Not only is the work environment punishing, but the challenges of trying to maintain a stable life in a fast-paced and competitive system are also daunting. The high social and environmental burden of capitalism is the reason we are moving toward a different system with a focus on sustainability and health, and it cannot come too soon for highly sensitive people.

There are a number of reasons why highly sensitive people struggle in a capitalistic system:

- HSPs want to do quality work. Quality work takes time. Capitalism is an impatient system and does not want to invest the time that HSPs want to invest to do satisfying work.

- Workers in a capitalistic system are expected to work at almost a machine-like pace. HSPs cannot sustain the pace energetically.

- Capitalism is highly competitive, pitting one against the other. HSPs are holistic so competitive practices do not resonate with them.

- Capitalism treats people like resources when people are more than commodities.

- Individuality is supported only to a degree. Capitalism invented the "economic man" but that does not mean that people have been free to be themselves as HSPs, minorities, and other-gendered people know.

Capitalism has brought many benefits but has also reduced human skills because many formerly human tasks have been shifted to machines. Some people have called it deskilling.[12] In fact most people's work supports the mechanized system, and as a result, most cannot survive without the products created by factories and offered in stores. The capitalistic system created a high degree of dependency on its automated production and distribution system. Not all of this is problematic. However when needs are met by machines, which use a finite resource like oil, it is necessary to consider change for the sake of our well-being.

The Energy Conflicts Of Highly Sensitive People

Highly sensitive people have more differences with others than just values. Their biology provides them with gifts and abilities that others do not have. Their sensitivity to nuance, as discussed in the "DOES" model, meant they can see what many miss and have important big-picture perspectives that can be useful. However, their unique perspective, which they develop from listening to the energies around them, is not always welcome.

12 Deskilling, Wikipedia, https://en.wikipedia.org/wiki/Deskilling

Because of their insights and wisdom, HSPs can be marginalized as a defensive move by others around them. This hazard can cause them to become defensive about sharing what they offer because they have learned that people are not always interested in hearing their truth and observations. Sometimes they cannot articulate what they notice—it may be a hunch or gut instinct—and until they have processed the information they take in, they will struggle to communicate their perceptions.

HSP sensitivity invites them to see where a framework is not working. Through their energy awareness, they can see the disconnects, missed information, and miscalculation. They see when relationships between people lack mutuality, care, and consideration. They notice how well all systems function and the condition of their natural environment. Highly sensitive people can be very sophisticated. Their insights can help create new possibilities at a time when the world is looking for new ideas and ways of being. HSPs have the ability to understand different frameworks like Spiral Dynamics and find ways to share their knowledge with others. Learning to communicate new possibilities is one of the biggest challenges and greatest opportunities for the highly sensitive.

HSP insights are especially important right now, as the limits and missteps of late-stage capitalism are becoming more evident and the world transitions to a new sustainable living model. Highly sensitive people can offer their perceptions as an aid to people struggling to make sense of what is happening and trying to make changes.

Aggression Is No Longer Enough

The human race has used force for thousands of years as an antidote to scarcity and violent opportunism. Although most of people dislike aggression, many consider it a necessary part of life. Now it is increasingly seen to be creating problems rather than solving them. Aggression can be a primitive reactive way of handling differences. As the world becomes more complicated, aggression cannot offer the solutions that create valuable and practical answers to current problems. It has outlived its usefulness.

Aggression is not a substitute for being present, being constructive, and creatively solving problems to support quality of life. With more than 7 billion people on the planet, aggression cannot be used to solve every problem.

Most people are seeking improved quality of life. It will take a lot of change to create the needed improvements. Aggression is a simplistic solution when more complex and insightful changes are needed. Increasingly aggression is being used by those who want to block progress and prevent solutions that join people in common problem solving.

In the modern world, aggression has sometimes served the objectives of economic growth. Resource wars are becoming more frequent. Capitalism dislikes limits and those who place limits on it since limitlessness is one of the foundational concepts of modern capitalism. In fact, if you say you cannot do something you bump into a bias against limits as evidenced by the extraordinary efforts of businesses to promote and protect their growth in the form of lobbying, tax breaks, and accounting practices. However, limits are real whether we like them or not. War cannot change the natural limits of nature to serve human needs and desires. A tree can be cut down and used, but once cut down it will take a long time to regenerate a new source of that wood.

Aggression does not overcome the natural processes that govern all of us. You can only wear one set of clothes, live in one place, and focus on one thing at a time. By refusing natural and physical limits, you destroy the physical world and yourself in an ongoing race for more. Aggression to serve such a destructive agenda needs to be changed because it is not constructive.

Highly sensitive people have the sensitivity to nuance that enables them to notice natural and systemic processes and their condition. That ability is desperately needed now as the world tries to get a handle on how capitalism has decreased our planet's sustainability. HSPs can seize this moment in time to become a part of the process of moving past outmoded cultural systems. They can promote inclusiveness and quality of life for everyone while working toward a more down-to-earth and sustainable way of life.

Competition And Resources

A competitive economy misuses resources. At one time, the balance between resources and the number of humans consuming them was such that people did not worry about the scarcity of natural resources the way we do now under climate change. In earlier times, transforming natural resources to meet unmet human needs was the critical issue. Fast forward to the present, at the end of the material age we have been living in, we have solved the problem of transforming raw materials into useful products. In the process of creating a higher standard of living, we have created huge, complex organizations and institutions, which consume a lot of resources to survive and succeed.

One of the features of competition is that a competitor is expected to be self sustaining—standing on his or her own two feet. It is a survival of the fittest mindset. Therefore all businesses and institutions worry about their survival and want to control as many resources as possible to ensure their survival. Capitalism creates a need to hoard. When people work under such fearful conditions, they can become shortsighted and forget about the needs of other people. Competition is not a coexistence model for human society, nor is it designed to support sustainability.

Competition, Resentment And Growth

Because of the resources required for effective competition, people rightfully understand that the deck is stacked against them unless they have a way to lay claim to the resources they need to compete effectively.

The human race is diverse in many ways including different levels of skills, knowledge, and opportunity. Unfortunately, the demands of competition mean that many have less access to resources they need to compete effectively. An article from Yes To Life No To Mining[13] lays out the problem of how mining operations consume or pollute so much of the water resources that the local farmers are unable to water their crops adequately. They become sick or are driven off their lands.

Feeling displaced is common in a competitive system where competition becomes more important than the well-being of people and the Earth. You do not have to be highly sensitive to feel marginalized in a competitive system. Naturally, people feel resentful when highly competitive institutions preempt their needs.

Furthermore, competition requires allies and supporters and therefore conformity to a set of values that serve the competitive system. If your values are different, you can be marginalized and find it hard to gain the traction you need to be successful.

Competition creates much harm.

Competition And HSP Emotional Pain

Highly sensitive people suffer a lot of emotional pain because of competition. Not only are HSPs unhappy with the adversarial nature of competition, they are unlikely to have the huge amounts of energy that effective competition requires. As a result, they often find that although they have a lot of talent and ability to offer, their nature and its limitations make it hard to mount the career effort that will enable them to rise to the top of their professions.

HSPs with a lot of support can succeed, but often the challenge of being highly sensitive in a hyper-fast world takes its toll and highly sensitive people can become ill. A highly sensitive person can lose their ability to do

13 Is Mining Really On Top In Africa, Yes To Life No To Mining, http://www.yestolifenotomining.org/is-mining-really-on-top-in-africa/

the kind of work they want and, if they expend the effort, may find that they have lost their health. It is a high price either way.

HSP sensitivity extends to the pain of others suffering in a competitive system which creates losses, feelings of exclusion, and the demoralizing effects of superficial values. Their empathy as outlined in the "DOES" model means that they are not isolated from the pain created by capitalism and will prefer behaviors and roles which do not add to it.

Competition And Self Abandonment

Many HSPs try to fit in because they need to survive. Survival choices whether for financial or other immediate concerns can cause HSPs serious stress and other health issues. Having been taught that there is something wrong with them, some HSPs think they must abandon or defer their own needs to address an immediate concern. The self-disregard required to survive in capitalistic work environments can result in long-term health problems as well as resentment and depression. Many highly sensitive people fear for their ability to take care of themselves in a world that values and rewards people who are not sensitive. Most HSPs struggle to find a place for themselves in the world where they can be their best, contribute according to their gifts, and be rewarded and valued.

Why Competition Cannot Continue In Its Present Form

Competition can stimulate action, but it is usually focused on the short term. Although competition has solved urgent material deficits for many human beings, addressing our physical needs has come at the price of significant social problems around discrimination and chronic health problems. The values of capitalism and the institutions that serve it have created a social space filled with conflict and distrust. Although distrust between humans is a long-standing problem that emerged long before capitalism, competition increases distrust because in a competitive system beating others is the objective. More and more people are now seeking ways to reduce and end the distrust that many think holds people hostage through movements promoting inclusion.

Fragile beginnings have caused distrust among people since scarcity was the norm of early human cultural life. Although many people are working on healing themselves from this legacy of distrust and scarcity and there is more understanding of the patterns of human life, society has not yet arrived at a place that asks, "How can we create cultures that are designed to foster trust?" That is coming and is an important next step for the human species.

A New Framework Is Necessary

Capitalism is a fear-based framework with a warlike competitive cultural structure that rewards the survivor. It is not accidental that "Survivor" is a popular reality television show. Capitalism has commodified people and nature in the interest of creating a higher standard of material comfort.

As people and nature struggle and decline under the weight of the demands of capitalism, a new framework is emerging. It has been in the works for some time under the radar. This new framework offers much hope for highly sensitive people and others who have been excluded. We will look at this new system next.

Turning To Joy

One of the upsides of materialism is that has been an important step in changing the typically human life from one of misery to greater joy. Materialism may not be joyful for highly sensitive people but even highly sensitive people like to have enough of the creature comforts that make life livable.

Material comforts are just one form of joy. There are many others including health, creating something worthwhile, doing for others, helping people heal, connection, and sharing. Many of those joys have been missing for a long time. Fortunately people are now shifting their attention to those neglected joys and are starting to create a world where they are possible.

CHAPTER 8

The Rise Of The "We" And The HSP Challenge

Out of necessity, the world is moving out of an economic and cultural model based on individualism and materialism into one based on community, inclusiveness, and sharing.

As you may have noticed, the Western capitalistic system dislikes social safety nets. Its hyper-individualism pits one person against another in an endless competition for resources and support to meet basic survival needs.

The New "We"

There is a new group consciousness emerging. The new "we" is creating a framework based on the "commons," the entire inheritance of shared natural and cultural resources and infrastructure. People will be able to share resources and no longer have to be totally self-contained in order to survive. This new approach will create an environment that promotes healthier interdependency—a more natural way of living.

The current model of total autonomy is expensive. If we each must own everything we need, we are contributing to an unsustainable consumption-based system. So extreme self reliance and absolute autonomy will have to give way to a new cultural model that promotes environmental sustainability and smart interdependence. The change has already begun.

Common Ground Matters

Striking a balance between the needs of the group and the needs of individuals has eluded the human race for a long time. The human race has not yet found a way to create a balance that supports the group and allows for individual self-expression in a fully constructive way. Society learns incrementally and has more self-governance lessons to come.

The extreme individualism of capitalism has caused harm to people's sense of community and trust, and to the shared community of Mother Earth. The harm to nature, the world's living home has to be rectified or humans will not survive as a species. To do that society will have to re-embrace community as the foundation of our living systems: physical and cultural.

Intelligent Differences

One reason cultures get out of balance is that they suppress important aspects of life to achieve a result. Materialism, which needs people to consume, discourages simple living, sharing, and other consumption-reducing ideas in favor of mass-produced goods and convenience. Capitalism makes income generation the most important activity so people leverage their time to make more money. If you are responsible for your autonomy in an uncertain world with no guarantees and few social supports, focusing on income is important and necessary.

Time has a commodity value in the capitalistic system—as the saying goes, "Time is money." People use money to accomplish a lot of things, including saving time, but at a high price. By supporting individualism, autonomy, and materialism at the expense of community, our capitalistic system is gradually destroying all our shared resources, including the environment, the most important support for human life.

It is important to recognize the human capacity to go from one extreme to another whether in creating community or promoting hyper-individualism. When a society asserts "we are all one," they acknowledge all that is shared but usually do so by denying the important realities of differences. As a result, they will shortchange themselves with a new imbalance between the self and the group. The two extremes are total control or total individuality:

- Fascist societies control all aspects of society and the individual is totally subordinated to the needs and agenda of the state. Such highly controlled societies marshal resources well and expect everyone to work together to advance state objectives.

- Late-stage capitalistic societies are considered hyper-individualized. Hyper-individualized societies have difficulty creating successful group efforts because citizens are not oriented toward team effort.

The animal kingdom seems to have this balance down. You would never hear a giraffe say, "I will not live in the same world as a mosquito," or an eel decide that all kangaroos have to go. They can all be part of the natural ecosystem and coexist at the same time.[14] We humans have a hard time living together in a balanced and balancing ecosystem.

This balance that humans have not yet achieved is one that highly sensitive people, with their energetic perceptual gifts, can help realize. HSPs notice when conformity in its rigidity overlooks and misses something. They notice when the cultural paradigm is on autopilot and causes damage. They notice imbalances. One of their gifts to the world can be helping it find a better balance between self and community.

How The Personal Development Movement Is Creating Space For HSPs And Change

One upside to capitalism is that in creating a system for producing necessary goods, it has generated opportunities for personal development that would not have been possible otherwise. It has brought:

- The opportunity for individuals to develop unique specialized skills and unique career paths. Many are finding it possible to

---

14 David Tillman, Causes, Consequences And Ethics Of Biodiversity, Nature, International Weekly Journal Of Science, May, 2000 http://www.nature.com/nature/journal/v405/n6783/full/405208a0.html

become successfully self-employed with their technical and specialized knowledge.

- Knowledge about patterns of behavior with the help of scientific research and computers, which has created new ideas about how to invest in compassionate action and suppress or rechannel aggressive tendencies.

- Mastery of the material needs of humans, which opens the door to new interests and stages of development leading to the end of materialism as the dominant task of society.

- An internet that democratizes the human voice so more people have a say in their lives.

- Inexpensive access to acquired knowledge through the internet, which gives more people the information they need so they can be successful in their lives.

Individual personal development improves not only living standards but also the ability of individuals to contribute their voices to political and cultural discussions. All over the world, personal development is making it possible for previously marginalized people to participate in the economic life of their countries. Even if you find many economic activities of questionable value, growing numbers of sophisticated people are causing social and economic changes unheard of in the past. Slow Money, localized economies, LGBT inclusion, and challenges to many forms of exclusion are happening now. These new movements are innovations and attempts to address the excesses and limitations of capitalism.

The process of personal development has brought fresh opportunities for marginalized talents, creating a path for inclusion and the movements for inclusion that are sweeping the globe. All of these efforts will help societies reduce fear-based systems as more and more people make known their desire for a fairer and healthier planet. Highly sensitive people are big beneficiaries of these changes.

The HSP Challenge

Although they have much to offer the world in this time of transition, highly sensitive people have been excluded for so long that they often struggle to find common ground with people who are different or more conforming than they are. Many HSPs are healing the wounds of competition, status seeking, put-downs, and other social ills of materialistic capitalism. Although highly sensitive people may dislike social isolation, social inclusion has not always been attractive either. Because of the damage many HSPs have sustained, their healing needs can be huge and an important part of their life journey.

Although HSPs have large healing needs, it would be of great value to the world if they could heal and take their place in the world after having been wounded and marginalized for so long. The world needs their deep process smarts and talent for nuances, as Elaine Aron has illuminated in the "DOES" model, to navigate the path to a new cultural model. The task of change is that big. It is likely that out of necessity HSP values of compassion will become the dominant values of the world. HSPs will become more at home in the world, have an easier time being accepted, and be more supported in their efforts to come into their own. If there was ever a time for highly sensitive people to end marginalization and isolation, it is now.

Highly sensitive people can make some important changes to participate more in this evolving world. Although they will be discussed later in the book, here is a preview of some of those changes:

- Do their healing inner work.

- Develop their skills and natural gifts.

- Learn collaborative group skills.

- Become skilled and accepting of human exchange systems involving money and other forms of trade.

- Develop lifestyles that support their optimal health.

- Get their needs met so that they are free to contribute effectively.

- Finding the place(s) where they want to contribute.

Why Me, Why Now?

It can be very difficult for highly sensitive people to heal from the traumas of living in a non-sensitive world. The aggression they experience causes many highly sensitive people to withdraw from the world. For many, healing their wounds is a lifelong journey, but it is only part of the story of the emergent highly sensitive person. HSPs are meant to be a part of the momentous changes taking place now. They deserve a healthy world, as does everyone else. Some might say that the time for highly sensitive people to take their place in the world is now. The world cannot wait, and HSPs cannot wait.

CHAPTER 9

The Trend Is Your Friend

Substantive change occurs when group consensus reaches a tipping point supporting change. Some trends have emerged over the past one hundred or more years that are shifting the balance toward a new cultural system that is more egalitarian, offering people new hope and a progressive path forward. What is fascinating is these movements are both local and global.

Globalization has been an economic event up until recently. It is now shifting and becoming a justice event as nations and economic entities have to give way to populist and environmental needs.

Survival has been the focus of human life for centuries, which is how long it has taken the human race to learn and develop the necessary survival tools and skills. The process has been messy but largely (too) successful; the human race has created substantial infrastructure to support human life. Throughout this journey, our species has rewarded those who have helped further survival. Enough structural resources exist now, which is creating a window of opportunity to shift our priorities from survival-based systems to sustainability-driven ones. There is a special opportunity for change and it is up to people to embrace it.

This following list of the most important emerging trends and movements can help highly sensitive people find suitable ways to direct their own work efforts in support of a better world. Additional information can be found in the Resources section.

The Commons Movement

According to David Bollier and Burns Weston, leaders of the emerging commons movement:

"The commons ... is a social system for the long-term stewardship of resources that preserves shared values and community identity.

Fortunately, the commons is not just an abstract idea. It's a living reality, thanks to millions of commoners around the world. People are managing forests, fisheries, irrigation water, urban spaces, creative works, knowledge and much else as commons. In so doing, they are in the vanguard of a new/old trend: using the social practices of commoning as a way to reclaim shared wealth while fighting the predatory behavior of neoliberal capitalism. The global commons movement is not a traditional movement defined by an ideology or policy agenda. It is united, rather, by its participants' commitment to certain social practices and principles of self-governance; commoners are passionate about self-organizing their own alternative models of provisioning to meet their basic needs in fair, inclusive and participatory ways."[15]

Biologist Garret Hardin denigrated the commons in an essay by in 1968, when he coined the phrase "the tragedy of the commons." He was not the first to disparage efforts at sharing resources; many throughout history who have done so. Fortunately the work of Professor Elinor Ostrom and her colleagues rectified the mischaracterization of the commons. Professor Ostrom won the Nobel Prize in Economics in 2009 for her life work showing that commons techniques are effective in managing and promoting viable, sustainable social systems for sustaining collective resources, especially those of nature.

The commons movement is built on a Commons Framework of belonging, co-creating, equity, sustainability, governance, interdependence,

---

15 David Bollier and Burns H. Weston, The Commons as a Growing Global Movement, CSR Wire, http://www.csrwire.com/blog/posts/1203-the-commons-as-a-growing-global-movement, January 31, 2014

and responsibility. It aims to protect and nurture our shared heritage of earth, air, water, cultural, and other human creations including public spaces and local communities.

One of the most important groups in the Commons Movement is The New Economy Coalition (NEC), an umbrella organization for many new economy organizations. It is headquartered in Boston, Massachusetts, and as of this writing has 122 organizations in its network including:

- The American Sustainable Business Council is creating a new vision and framework for economic development that creates prosperity, sustainability, and social justice.

- 350.org is the environmental action powerhouse created by Bill McKibben.

- "The Caring Economy Campaign "connects the dots between care and prosperity, showing the value of care in economic terms to support new patterns of investment in human growth and development."

- The Center For Social Inclusion focuses on transforming structural inequity and exclusion into structural fairness and inclusion.

- CitySeed is leading the effort to develop sustainable local food supplies.

- Community Sourced Capital creates innovative financial systems for communities so that local businesses can receive the financial support that they need.

- Democracy Collaborative wants to change the prevailing paradigm of economic development—and of the economy as a whole—toward a new emphasis and system based on shared ownership and stewardship of resources and workplaces and sustainable community.

- Fair World Project promotes equitable economies, which respect and support the dignity of people and nature.

- Institute For Local Self Reliance is a hands-on designer of sustainable community in partnership with communities and their organizations.

- Living Economies Forum focuses on creating and fostering the tools for local cooperative self organization.

- Post Growth Institute seeks paths to prosperity that do not rely on the unsustainable growth model.

- Shareable is an online hub for the sharing movement.

There is room for a wide variety of highly sensitive people in the New Economy of all skills and abilities. Some people are creating the legal framework for a global commons that protects all natural and cultural resources for all. Others are working at the local level creating working groups to handle specific commons issues. Water, pollution, local food, and claiming local cultural resources are some examples. Some are lending technical skills and other interpersonal, healing, and administrative skills. Some roles are activist roles, other are contemplative or nurturing. There are many ways HSPs can participate in the life redefining movement.

The Relocalization Movement

The relocalization movement could be called the sustainable communities movement. Its purpose is to build resilience at the local level so people have more confidence that their basic needs can be met.

The relocalization movement is where the action happens on the ground. Where the New Economy is often about creating a legal and structural framework, the relocalization movement gets its hands dirty.

Resilient communities create and maintain resources to meet ongoing basic local needs. Resilient communities reduce survival fear by tackling the issues around resilience when they lay the foundation for a resilience process and structure, which supports community members through the ups and downs of life.

According to leading resilience leader, Post Carbon Institute:

> Relocalization is a strategy to build societies based on the local production of food, energy and goods, and the local development of currency, governance and culture. The main goals of relocalization are to increase community energy security, to strengthen local economies, and to improve environmental conditions and social equity. The relocalization strategy developed in response to the environmental, social, political and economic impacts of global over-reliance on cheap energy.[16]

Resilience in this context is:

> ...commonly defined as the capacity of a system to absorb disturbance and re-organize while undergoing change so as to still retain essentially the same function, structure, identity, and feedbacks. Resilience is a rich and complex concept. It has roots in systems theory, and it has a variety of interpretations and applications including for ecosystems management, disaster preparedness, and even community planning.[17]

Communities are currently dependent on an economic system that concentrates resources in the hands of a few and distributes them from

16 Post Carbon Institute, http://www.postcarbon.org/relocalize/
17 Post Carbon Institute, http://www.postcarbon.org/relocalize/

centralized facilities to locations around the world. This system relies on cheap, irreplaceable fossil fuels. Resilient communities recognize the need to develop their local resources so people can take care of themselves independent of the availability of fossil fuels for providing their food and other goods.

Resilient communities are the local focal point of the commons movement. They protect a community's dependencies, especially natural resources and basic needs: water, air, ecosystem health, food, and health.

The relocalization movement has been fostered by two interrelated organizations:

- Post Carbon, which researches and disseminates information about peak oil and life after carbon fuels including a local resilience initiative.

- The Transition Network, which trains people in creating resilient communities. It has over 1100 communities within its network.

The resilient communities movement is a great opportunity for highly sensitive people to connect with their community around values that mesh with HSP compassion and empathy. Creating resilient communities is a compassionate thing to do. There are many ways to participate: creating community gardens, creating cooperatives around food and healing, and restoring the local environment.

The Slow Movement: Quality Over Quantity

According to Wikipedia, the Slow Movement began in 1986:

> The Slow Movement advocates a cultural shift toward slowing down life's pace. It began with Carlo Petrini's protest against the opening of a McDonald's restaurant in Piazza di Spagna, Rome in 1986 that sparked the creation of the Slow Food organization. Over time, this developed into a

subculture in other areas, such as Cittaslow (Slow Cities), Slow Living, Slow Travel, and Slow Design.[18]

Norwegian philosopher Guttorm Fløistad expressed the intention and spirit of the Slow Movement:

> The only thing for certain is that everything changes. The rate of change increases. If you want to hang on you had better speed up. That is the message of today. It could however be useful to remind everyone that our basic needs never change. The need to be seen and appreciated! It is the need to belong. The need for nearness and care, and for a little love!

> This is given only through slowness in human relations. In order to master changes, we have to recover slowness, refection and togetherness. There we will find real renewal.[19]

The Slow Movement is a transformation movement that seeks to show how we can take what we have and live better. It suggests that negative perceptions about slowness are causing us to deplete ourselves with poor quality, relationships, sloppy learning, and work.[20]

Many highly sensitive people have received negative feedback for being slow. However, because they are sensitive they notice the costs of going too fast and resist the fast pace of modern culture. The Slow Movement is an opportunity for HSPs to live at their correct pace and find partners as well as colleagues with a similar approach to life and work.

The Slow Movement addresses the time poverty of modernity but more importantly the desire for connection and the desire to lead a connected life with families, communities, home, and the natural environment.

---

18 Wikipedia, Slow Movement, https://en.wikipedia.org/wiki/Slow_Movement

19 Wikipedia, Slow Movement, https://en.wikipedia.org/wiki/Slow_Movement

20 Movimiento Slow, History And Philosophy, http://movimientoslow.com/en/flosofa.html

People who have embraced the Slow Movement can be good companions for highly sensitive people. They are likely to respect the deep processing of highly sensitive people: the "D" of the "DOES" model. It is worth investigating the Slow Movement if you are thinking of creating a business or a service. How do you integrate Slow Movement ideas into your work? What support systems do you need to create space for contemplative management? How do you set reasonable limits so your business thrives? What is your "stake in the ground," the focus of your work that lets you be slow, thorough, and successful?

Connected World: The Rise Of The Amateur And The Maker Movement

Technology has created flexible options for people to live and work. The internet is a huge aggregation of shared knowledge and information. It is the largest library in the world and the largest accumulation of active human voices. As a result, anyone can have a voice online. Talented people now have access to the ears of the larger world. The middlemen and gatekeepers who could have blocked or torpedoed their efforts in the past have less power and control. Self-educated people can find a place for themselves in the online world.

- Technology has helped people who are musicians and writers find an audience for their work. Many people now use technology to create audio, video, and films. The viral nature of the internet makes   sharing work possible by eliminating commercial gatekeepers who made and controlled markets.

- The internet makes it possible for individuals to share their wisdom and support themselves doing so. It is a repository of the communal knowledge base inside of and outside of mainstream education which anyone can access. Since the world moves so fast, being up-to-date often means going online.

- Experts in their fields are creating courses available to the wider world. As a result, more and more schools are accessing the internet as a teaching aid. Why not have the best teachers you can have for your students? Sometimes online education is the source of the most knowledgeable teachers.

Highly sensitive people can take advantage of the democratization of information by setting up knowledge businesses. Online businesses offer schedule flexibility, which can give an HSP the pacing they need to be successful.

Social Entrepreneurship

Ashoka, the largest network of social entrepreneurs in the world, describes the social entrepreneur this way:

> Just as entrepreneurs change the face of business, social entrepreneurs act as the change agents for society, seizing opportunities others miss to improve systems, invent new approaches, and create solutions to change society for the better. While a business entrepreneur might create entirely new industries, a social entrepreneur develops innovative solutions to social problems and then implements them on a large scale.[21]

Social entrepreneurship uses the technologies of business and markets to handle and transform the large-scale issues of the Commons and the unaddressed issues of social equity. Unlike commercial business that seeks short-term profit, which often creates social problems, social enterprises tackle big social issues and have a long-term view.

The profit that social entrepreneurs seek is the social profit of greater equity and their purpose is to create permanent, long-term change.

There is disagreement about the definition of a social entrepreneur. Some people include social activists and others do not. What they all

---

21 What Is A Social Entrepreneur? Ashoka.org https://www.ashoka.org/social_entrepreneur

have in common is that they tackle big challenges involving significant unmet needs. Here are a few examples from the Forbes List Of 30 Top Entrepreneurs:

- Jordan Kassalow, an optometrist by training, runs an organization that sells ready-made reading glasses to people in the developing world.

- Sam Goldman and Ned Tozun, of D.Light Design, manufacture inexpensive lamps and sell them in communities that don't have reliable electricity.

- Tom Skazy dropped out of Princeton University to create Terracycle, which sells fertilizer and over two hundred fifty products made from sixty waste streams.

- Jane Chen's company manufactures a sleeping bag-like device called the "Thermpod," which warms low-birth weight babies in hospitals and clinics that have unreliable electricity and heat lamps that don't always work. [22]

Highly sensitive people often find business cultures to be too aggressive and fast paced to suit them. In addition, corporate interests may not mesh with humanistic HSPs. Social entrepreneurship is a way to create an enterprise—and it does not have to be a big one—with a humanistic intent and is a possible career path for sensitives with an interest in entrepreneurial work.

Reshaping Capitalism: The Sharing Movement And Others

We live in late-stage capitalism, which means that capitalism is evolving into a new system. There are many ways that the new system is manifesting, some of which have been discussed. Capitalism identifies with the private and the individual. Its story is about the accumulation of wealth.

22 Forbes List Of 30 Top Entrepreneurs, Forbes, http://www.forbes.com/sites/helencoster/2011/11/30/forbes-list-of-the-top-30-social-entrepreneurs/

The new system will be about the collective, the new emerging "we," sharing and the accumulation of social good will.

One manifestation of change is the sharing movement sometimes called the Sharing Economy.

According to People Who Share:

> The Sharing Economy is a socio-economic ecosystem built around the sharing of human and physical resources. It includes the shared creation, production, distribution, trade and consumption of goods and services by different people and organizations.
>
> The Sharing Economy encompasses the following aspects: swapping, exchanging, collective purchasing, collaborative consumption, shared ownership, shared value, co-operatives, co-creation, recycling, upcycling, re-distribution, trading used goods, renting, borrowing, lending, subscription based models, peer-to-peer, collaborative economy, circular economy, pay-as-you-use economy, wikinomics, peer-to-peer lending, micro financing, micro-entrepreneurship, social media, the Mesh, social enterprise, futurology, crowdfunding, crowdsourcing, cradle-to-cradle, open source, open data, user generated content (UGC).[23]

The Sharing Economy will be one of the most important tools for healing the planet and people from the destructive impacts of extractive capitalism. It will foster a better use of resources so more attention can be given to environmental and healing needs while still supporting quality of life.

Consumption will no longer be the primary economic activity and social identities will not be tied to our accumulation. But people still need to eat and live. Sharing what has been created will support life while reducing human impacts on the planet.

23 What Is The Sharing Economy, People Who Share, http://www.thepeoplewhoshare.com/blog/what-is-the-sharing-economy/

Sharing offers a lot of possibilities for HSPs to work and connect. Because there are so many ways to share, HSPs have many ways to participate in the sharing world. An advantage for sensitives is that sharing lets them minimize their expenses so that they can be free to pursue their passions and purpose. There are many sharing organizations already set up, and they can be created in any local community. See the resource section for additional information.

Compassion, Compassionate Cities, And The Equity Movements

Compassion is becoming a mainstream value as demonstrated by the Compassionate Cities project. Seventy-two cities are becoming or already are Compassionate Cities/Regions.

In 2008, religious scholar Karen Armstrong received a TED prize to create the Charter For Compassion. Two years later, the International Campaign For Compassionate Cities began with a visit from the Dalai Lama. Within a short period of time, the charter has been adopted by Appleton, Wisconsin; Basalt, Colorado; Lake County, California; London, Ontario in Canada; and Seattle, Washington. Canada is working to become the first Compassionate Country and New Delhi the first city in Asia.

There are no out-of-pocket costs to start a Compassionate City—just the commitment to bringing the value of compassion to the community.

Compassionate Cities begin by signing on to the Charter for Compassion. It is an impressive pledge. This is what it contains:

> The principle of compassion lies at the heart of all religious, ethical and spiritual traditions, calling us always to treat all others as we wish to be treated ourselves. Compassion impels us to work tirelessly to alleviate the suffering of our fellow creatures, to dethrone ourselves from the centre of our world and put another there, and to honour the inviolable sanctity of every single human being, treating everybody, without exception, with absolute justice, equity and respect.

It is also necessary in both public and private life to refrain consistently and empathically from inflicting pain. To act or speak violently out of spite, chauvinism, or self-interest, to impoverish, exploit or deny basic rights to anybody, and to incite hatred by denigrating others—even our enemies—is a denial of our common humanity. We acknowledge that we have failed to live compassionately and that some have even increased the sum of human misery in the name of religion.

We therefore call upon all men and women to restore compassion to the centre of morality and religion ~ to return to the ancient principle that any interpretation of scripture that breeds violence, hatred or disdain is illegitimate ~ to ensure that youth are given accurate and respectful information about other traditions, religions and cultures ~ to encourage a positive appreciation of cultural and religious diversity ~ to cultivate an informed empathy with the suffering of all human beings—even those regarded as enemies.

We urgently need to make compassion a clear, luminous and dynamic force in our polarized world. Rooted in a principled determination to transcend selfishness, compassion can break down political, dogmatic, ideological and religious boundaries. Born of our deep interdependence, compassion is essential to human relationships and to a fulfilled humanity. It is the path to enlightenment, and indispensable to the creation of a just economy and a peaceful global community. [24]

Notice the deep respect at the heart of the Charter for Compassion.

Compassion is an essential drive for all of the equity movements: animal rights, environmental sustainability, human rights, gender and transgender acceptance, etc. These individual compassion campaigns have been working independently for a long time. Charter For Compassion, http://charterforcompassion.org/sign-share-charter

---

24 Charter For Compassion, http://charterforcompassion.org/sign-share-charter

When the Compassionate City movement came along, it started making compassion a foundational part of a place to cover all community members. To have compassion tied to a place is very new.

There are many other initiatives that fall under the compassion movement: fair trade, fair wage, the right to health care, end of life compassion. Some initiatives are local and others are global. An important takeaway is the critical mass of compassionate action that is taking place. We are reaching the point of no return on this long awaited desire for a world that is compassionate and livable.

Compassionate Cities could be interesting places for HSPs to live and work. Those who are interested could even start creating a compassionate city where they live.

The Process Of Change

Hierarchical organizational styles that served us in the past are outmoded. Although they made sense in early human societies when information and knowledge were scarce, power concentrated in the hands of those few who decide for the group/tribe no longer serves the wellbeing of people in complex cultures. Group elites too often enjoy their privileged positions at the expense of others. Human cultural systems evolved around these early management structures and we have continued them for thousands of years. Now information and knowledge are abundant. Thanks to the internet and self-improvement, many people are becoming more self governing and learning to work collaboratively with others. Abraham Maslow's self-actualizing person has been a beacon and a compass for many people since he introduced the idea in the 1950s and '60s. As a result, self-improvement is now an approximately $10 billion industry in the United States alone.

The human race has been preparing for change for some time. Huge numbers of people are doing their healing and ascension work through psychological and other forms of therapy like reiki and bodywork, 12-Step programs and organizations like Hay House. Transition groups are active throughout the world, and small community efforts are yielding important changes in local food supplies and neighbor collaboration.

People will be freeing themselves from a top-down world as they learn to create more together through:

- localized economies

- sharing

- a new connection with nature

- humanitarian-focused cultural systems.

Many changes have been underway for one hundred fifty years or more below the radar of large media and institutions but will gather momentum this century. We know this from the Spiral Dynamics chart earlier in the book, which showed that the egalitarian and humanistic system began about one hundred fifty years ago. Major shifts take time to develop. The egalitarian movement, which suits HSPs perfectly, is beginning to flower. This transition could still take hundreds of years to become established because it is a monumental shift in human attitudes, priorities, habits, and ways of life.

The world is finally becoming ready for highly sensitive people. We have to be ready to meet this momentous moment in human history that needs our wisdom, depth, and conscientiousness. We will now explore what that means.

SECTION 4: CLAIMING AGENCY

Overview

Elaine Aron's "DOES" model discusses the challenges of overstimulation for highly sensitive people. Because highly sensitive people take in so much information, they not only become overstimulated but they also have difficulty making choices about what actions to take. HSPs want to make decisions that have integrity and reflect their authenticity. Frameworks like Spiral Dynamics provide much-needed perspective on how the world is organized to make it easier to identify and separate our energy and problems from others. Reducing overwhelm creates space to be more active in the world. Claiming agency, which Merriam-Webster defines as, "the capacity, condition, or state of acting or of exerting power," is about using your gifts to serve the world, which is an important need and growth opportunity for the highly sensitive person.

CHAPTER 10

The Highly Sensitive Person: Perfect For The Times

Sometimes highly sensitive people compare themselves to non-HSPs and feel at a disadvantage. However, perceptions about highly sensitive people will change as they perfect their skills and effectiveness as compassionate guides for this transition time. The ways HSPs have been of value in the past—and to some degree the present—will become needed again as human culture re-embraces community, sharing, and nature.

Once upon a time HSPs were treasured for:

- being excellent trackers for tribes and other groups.

- shamanic, spiritual and healing skills.

- their creativity; many artists, writers and composers throughout history have been highly sensitive people. (Albert Einstein, Carl Jung, Jane Goodall, Abraham Lincoln, Dalai Lama, Eleanor Roosevelt, Elton John, Robin Williams, Nicole Kidman, Steve Martin, Orson Welles, and Alanis Morissette are just a few.)[25]

- being conscientious, which led them to work in many trades. Trades are a perfect way to channel and combine sensitivity and conscientiousness.

- their capacity to see into processes as troubleshooters and problem solvers.

25 Jim Hallowes, Albert Einstein, Nicole Kidman: Jim Hallowes Lists Famous Highly Sensitive People, Genconnect, November, 2010, http://www.genconnect.com/albert-einstein-nicole-kidman-jim-hallowes-list-of-famous-highly-sensitive-people/

A New Relationship With Nature And Time

Throughout most of human history, humans lived closely aligned with nature. Daily rhythms were in tune with natural rhythms because people lived off the land. In the past, although HSPs have always had to contend with the issue of being different, the life rhythms of social groups were not alien to sensitive energy, which meant that HSPs could share their special relationship with nature with others as a way to connect and take part in their social group.

However, with the Industrial Revolution, the human relationship with time and nature changed. Time in the modern age became a factor in the cost of production and so had a monetary value. Time and nature became separated as business turned nature into a commodity to be used for economic gain.

The Industrial Revolution also brought with it a different energy. If you listen to the current energetic rhythm of the capitalistic world, it has a mechanized, pounding quality to it like a machine. It does not have the wavelike dancing rhythms of nature. Machine energy and machine imagery have dominated the world for centuries now. Expressions like "artistic production" prove how much our living energy has become aligned with the mechanized world of business.

People's relationship to time and nature will change as the world shifts from late-stage capitalism as the dominant cultural system of the world to a new economic, and cultural system based on sustainability and saving the planet emerges, as shown in the chart on Spiral Dynamics in the Frameworks Section.[26] [27]Profit, growth, and a refusal to accept limits will fall by the wayside as misguided values as inclusion, healing, caring for people, the planet, and all its creatures become mainstream. This is not fanciful thinking or idealism. All change comes from necessity and an

26   Paul Mason, The End Of Capitalism Has Begun, Alternet, July 2015 http://www.alternet.org/economy/end-capitalism-has-begun

27   FJ White, Modern Capitalism's Death Spiral, Citizen Action Monitor, April, 2015, https://citizenactionmonitor.wordpress.com/2015/04/20/modern-capitalisms-death-spiral/

urgent need for the healing of Earth, people, and animals is driving this change.

Although highly sensitive people have to be careful to avoid the still toxic areas of our culture, we can now find more places where we can easily participate:

- Healing professions, especially alternative health.

- Counseling and coaching, which are increasingly online. HSPs are natural students and can share their wisdom online at a pace that works for their sensitive natures.

- Software and application development for the technically inclined, as the internet offers many opportunities in this field.

- Scientific and engineering fields, especially those investigating sustainability solutions could be promising.

- Creative roles, as the internet releases creatives from the obstacle of institutional gatekeepers. As a result, crafting and making things including food will become important pursuits as more and more people join the maker movement to express their talents and achieve greater control over their lives through self reliance.

- Social entrepreneurship is hot and will continue to be as solutions to the big problems of inequality are found.

- Legal, management and financial professionals for the commons and localizations movements that are creating new infrastructures and community groups as part of a larger effort to meet human basic needs locally and preserve the commons.

All of these areas can be perfect for highly sensitive people from a values perspective, provided the work environment is a healthy one. Highly sensitive people require work environments that are socially healthy, humane, and constructive if they are to function well.

The social, economic and environmental complexity we now live with will not go away. The complex organizations that we have for managing the infrastructure of human society will require deft and able management. Because HSPs have an innate talent for perceiving nuances, they can be very helpful for managing our complex systems and creating solutions to problems.

So how can HSPs participate effectively?

Becoming The Shift

It is great to have grand visions for the future, and as highly sensitive people with our holistic perspective, we can see the need for change.

But many HSPs know they do not control the world and therefore cannot force change; change has to occur one step at a time because this major transition will happen not only in individuals but also in all living systems. In order for the human race to embrace sustainable living, new systems and institutions have to be built based on the emerging collaborative skills people build in themselves. It will happen but it is a big shift which will take many generations to bring to fruition.

That is good news actually because we can join the process rather than feel too responsible for it—something HSPs are prone to do as discussed in the "DOES" model section on Empathy.

So what does this huge change mean for highly sensitive people? How do HSPs come out of hiding into a world that is still oriented toward aggression to be a part of the shift to compassionate and sustainable living without hurting ourselves? That is the challenge!

Human culture is evolving to a new human framework which has greater synchronicity with the highly sensitive person and the natural flow of life:

- HSP values will be mirrored in the cultural systems being created.

- HSPs will no longer be marginalized.

- Sensitive people will be respected for their gifts, which will be vital to the success of this transition.

- HSPs will have an easier time making a living.

- Highly sensitive people will have an easier time socially as more and more people show themselves to be kindred spirits.

However, HSPs still have to figure out how to interject themselves and participate in this change process. To take part effectively in this evolving world, they have to discover the way their sensitivity can be of value, acknowledge how it is misunderstood, and locate those interests and groups that serve the emerging sustainability and accept their values.

Self Trust: Becoming Comfortable In Your Own Skin

For many, being comfortable in your own skin means being accepted and knowing yourself to be acceptable to others. Acceptance from others is not readily available to highly sensitive people, so self-acceptance can be more challenging. Because HSPs receive so many conflicting messages about themselves, they can have a hard time seeing themselves clearly.

Self-acceptance and self-trust are not the same thing. You can accept yourself as you are; knowing that you are biologically different helps. However it is difficult to achieve self-trust if you cannot navigate the world effectively. Many highly sensitive people think less of themselves because they have difficulty processing what they take in and then figuring out what to do with that information in a timely manner. In a fast-paced world, it can be hard for a highly sensitive person to respond spontaneously to daily interactions with others. An HSP's processing needs are actually healthy, but he or she may see them and others may see them as a block.

Most highly sensitive people have a strong spiritual/humanitarian core, which helps them make decisions; using their natural humanity for decision-making can be wise and helpful. However, deep down, HSPs know there is more to it and wonder if they are not missing something that would make it easier to relate to others in a way that leaves them feeling satisfied.

Because of their nature highly sensitive people need:

- time to process energetic information

- awareness and social skills for handling the situations they find themselves in

- enough successful experience so that they can feel confident about their ability to be effective.

Not everyone admires kindness, as HSPs discover early in life. Your kindness can cause you to process deeply and seek the solutions and outcomes that offer the greatest goodness, which takes time, something the world may not allow you.

Fast is not kind.

Fast is not thorough.

Fast is not complete.

HSPs often feel of disappointed about the aggression in the world when they can see compassionate choices that are overlooked. Because they feel responsible, they can carry a lot of shame about their inability to be more effective. Since the world still shames kindness, HSPs can feel that their core nature is wrong. Even if they do not buy into the cultural story about the necessity and value of aggression, they nonetheless live in a world whose story differs from their own and through the wonders of consensus is more validated that theirs.

Healing From Aggression

Aggression does a lot of harm. In order to succeed, it has to justify the harm that is being done. It has to rationalize abuse.

Highly sensitive people cannot kid themselves about abuse. Well, actually they can try, but that is simply adding another injury to the first one. It simply does not work because HSP energetic systems are not fooled.

The world of aggression misses a lot. It makes a lot of mistakes because it is so focused on achieving a certain result that it fails to consider the wisdom of its desires. As a result it misses that:

- perspective equals power. Power does not come from your weapons. It comes from the ability to stand back, consider what is necessary and important, and decide on that basis. Perspective is an important part of real power.

- depth equals wisdom. A high-speed world by its very nature is going to be superficial because it is going too fast to consider long-term consequences. As a result, it makes high-speed choices, which can be very short-sighted.

- creativity equals choice. When you can stand back and consider the long-term implications of what you are doing, choices become available to you that are not possible when you are being overly aggressive and short-sighted.

Most of the cherished values of the highly sensitive person are peripheral to the current economic model. Fortunately, as has already been explored, a new, more inclusive world is developing and working its way to center stage. HSPs can participate in the development of the world that makes compassion one of its highest values.

Although the world of aggression does not want to hear about the wisdom of compassion, in a complex world, compassion serves the greater good. It means avoiding mindless competition. Serving the greater good with compassion creates hope for everyone.

The values that were shamed in the current economic system will become valued in the new one so one of our most important tasks is to heal the shame messages you have received which imply, overtly or covertly, that you are defective. This can be done through meditation, releasing/forgiveness exercises and journaling, or a process of self-appreciation that restores self-value. Through healing, you reclaim our natural goodness so that you can turn our sensitivity into an asset.

CHAPTER 11

The Importance Of Agency:
How To Turn Sensitivity Into An Asset

Highly sensitive people have great hearts and big-picture visions. They have a lot of awareness. However, there is something missing and that something makes it hard for HSPs to be effective and live the lives they want.

HSPs have trouble claiming their agency and using it. Agency is your ability to use your gifts in the world; it is the claiming of your power in the best sense of the word. The HSP nervous system takes in so much that it is hard to know what to do with it. It is hard to process all the information so you can make timely decisions. HSPs are conscientious, deep processors as discussed in the "DOES" model section, so you are not satisfied with quick fixes, reckless choices, and the easy way out.

Your agency is compromised by your hyperactive nervous systems so you may often feel defeated simply from being the sensitive person that you are. Being sensitive makes agency more complicated. It can inform and make you wiser, but the task of processing your sensitive information may cause you to put others before yourself to avoid creating harm. Caring for others suits the HSP empathetic natures and eases the loneliness you often feel, but over-caring is not a healthy solution.

Being aware of your sensitivity, figuring out where you belong and what work suits and interests you are important but just the beginning. Recognizing the limits of your energy, you need to develop the skills and supports that enable you to live a life that suits you, lets you be yourself, and serves your intentions.

Approaches For Claiming Agency

Here are some approaches that will help you find better solutions and be more effective:

- Using a holistic ecological framework like the Whole Self framework of Bill Plotkin to develop clarity of vision and your natural maturity. We will explore this framework soon.

- Developing the power of empathetic creativity.

- Discovering new ways to think about purpose.

- Learning the baby-step method of living well.

- Using the before and after tool for problem solving and progress.

- Becoming comfortable with self assertion and the safety of constructive action.

- Understanding the value of context-driven choices.

- Tuning in to process as bridge.

The Whole Self: A Holistic Ecological Framework

One advantage of being highly sensitive is that HSPs have a big-picture perspective. As a result, they are able to see beyond their own immediate concerns and can consider the implications of choices into the future. You could think of it as a transpersonal perspective.

This big-picture perspective and all of the information the HSP nervous system takes in give the sensitive person more information to consider about any topic or issue. It lets HSPs look at any issue from other perspectives, making it difficult to operate only from narrow interests.

Having so much information is great, but you still need tools for making decisions and setting priorities. HSPs have a special need for ways to handle the information they taken in to avoid overload. Finding ways to sort through information and possibilities in making choices is an important task for highly sensitive people. Frameworks are an important way to do that because they provide an easy-to-grasp skeleton of processes, structures, and concepts that makes processing information easier.

Spiral Dynamics, discussed in the Framework Section is an excellent example. Another useful framework for highly sensitive people is the Whole Self: a holistic ecological framework developed by depth psychologist Bill Plotkin and based on the wheel of life and nature as a process for development.

The Whole Self framework provides a way for people to understand themselves and their personal development in relation to nature. In other words, Dr. Plotkin proposes that our natural connection is with nature and not culture; therefore we can only become whole by relocalizing ourselves in terms of nature. He draws on the accumulated wisdom of many ecologically oriented sages in sharing this important path to wholeness and joy. A few of the many experts he cites are:

- soul poets like Ranier Maria Rilke

- Joseph Campbell

- ecophilosophers like Joanna Macy and Arne Naess

- Thomas Berry

- ecoliteracy advocates Richard Lewis and David Orr

- nature-based human developmental models offered by Dolores LaChapelle

- ecological imagineer and wilderness explorer Geneen Maria Haugen

- Carl Jung, Marion Woodman, and Robert Johnson

- numerous other anthropologists and psychologists with insights into nature-based human development.[28]

Bill Plotkin's framework is a tool that explains how you move through the various stages of life in a nature-centered way and ways you can become derailed from your natural progression through life. The Whole Self framework is organized by the four directions (north, south, east, and west), the seasons they represent, and how those seasons relate to important stages of our development. It offers archetypes to help you understand the gifts of each stage of life, the purpose of each stage, and exercises to develop your whole self.

The Whole Self framework is important because it is a useful tool for understanding yourself and others so that you can find constructive ways to relating and working. Dr. Plotkin offers the Nurturing Generative Adult as the example of nature-based maturity, which is a useful model for highly sensitive people seeking to grow into the best version of themselves.

Because Dr. Plotkin's work also shows how people can become derailed from the natural progression of their lives, HSPs can use the Whole Self model to understand the people they may find difficult to relate to. Learning this framework provides HSPs many useful insights into human development and as a result helps them detach from a lot of toxic energy around them.

The Power Of Empathetic Creativity

Empathy is a great tool of discovery. It lets you learn about the world because it helps you look at anything from another perspective. Empathy helps you understand all the information that your nervous system takes

28 Bill Plotkin, Nature And The Human Soul, 2008, p.57.

in. It helps you relate to the energy of each piece of information and if it is a multifaceted energy, you can engage all of it.

Empathy lets you into the complexity and nuance of the energy you take in so that you are able to perceive the dynamics and structure of anything. Empathy supports the deep processing that highly sensitive people are known for.

Highly sensitive people can use the insights they gain through their empathy to enrich their creativity. The deep processing that HSPs do leads to insights that then generate new solutions and possibilities in many areas of life.

Empathy will tell you what needs to be created. If you are wondering about a choice, your empathy and the energy you are experiencing can lead you to effective decisions. Empathy makes your net a little bigger by offering new possibilities through your energy experience and helps you understand what solutions will work in a given situation. As a result, it can be both a tool for creating excellence and for self-protection.

Exploring Purpose

It is common to frame purpose in life in terms of fitting into your culture. Since all humans are social beings, fitting in can feel good and help you to feel like you are part of the world. If you do not fit in, how do you find our purpose   and your place?

One way is to look to your natural gifts. For highly sensitive people, healing, teaching, and spiritual purposes often resonate.

Another way to look at purpose is to enlarge your focus by asking what natural talents do you offer and where are they needed or of value. In asking this question, you can develop ideas for a work or career path.

You can take your questioning one step further and ask, "How do my gifts help the evolution of the world at this point and into the future?" This question can give you a long-term arc of time for investing in a body of work. It can also be used to seek out people who are doing the same thing you are and that will help you find kindred spirits.

The Baby-Step Method Of Living Well

If you do not have big goals, the world may treat you like a failure. The idea that bigness is goodness has been around for a while and so accepted that people fall down and worship at the altar of bigness whether it is of value or not. Society has provided societal and economic supports for bigness and the creation of giants of all kinds. Bigness is associated with optimism and greatness, although they are not the same thing. Greatness exists even in small acts.

Being highly sensitive means that we can energetically see greatness. We can also see hollow bigness. The demand for bigness is a burden for highly sensitive people who have their hands full processing the energy downloads in our environments. HSPs are sensitive to all the ways that bigness doesn't work: the cost of bigness in resources and human time and attention, the inflexibility of the bigness mindset and its unresponsiveness to the ever-varying nature of daily life.

Big ambition as an end unto itself does not usually resonate with HSPs. There is a better way to work and contribute: the Baby-Step Method Of Living Well. Baby steps are an important tool for managing life in a sane way. Baby steps let you live in process—the ongoing flow of life— with all other creatures and listen to feedback from your environment and your inner voice as you progress through each day and your life. A baby step, process-oriented approach to life is right-brained. It avoids all of the errors of linear thinking. Making small steps minimizes the chances for catastrophic failure while letting you make adjustments as you progress. As a result, you can treat life like the learning experience it is without undue risk.

Taking baby steps let you absorb your energetic information and interact with life in a constructive way. It is healthy and sane and can help you avoid the burnout that comes from being over-ambitious.

There are many examples of people who use small acts to make change:

- One of the most famous examples is Rosa Parks who on December 1, 1955, in Montgomery, Alabama, refused to give up her seat in the colored section to a white passenger, after the white section was filled. This one small action led to her arrest, bus boycotts in her community, creation of a new community organization, MIA run by Martin Luther King, Jr., and a three hundred eighty-one-day boycott of the buses. At the time a case was pending at the Supreme Court regarding bus segregation. Although Rosa Parks was not a part of the case, the court affirmed the right of blacks on buses and bus segregation became illegal.[29]

- Another well-known example of small actions making a difference is the practice of microlending to help poor people develop a business that will support them and their families. Although there have been microlending activities in the past, one of the most famous examples is the Grameen Bank, founded in 1983 by Mohammed Yunus. Yunus, who was a Fulbright Scholar and graduate of Vanderbilt Business School, saw the need and opportunity to help people in his native Bangaldesh by making small loans. In 1976, Mr. Yunus obtained a loan from a government bank to start microlending. By 1982 he had 28,000 members. The following year he opened Grameen Bank and by July 2007 had issued US$6.38 billion to 7.4 million borrowers, many of whom were women. He was awarded the Ashoka: Innovators for the Public Global

---

29 Wikipedia, https://en.wikipedia.org/wiki/Rosa_Parks

Academy Member in 2001 and the Nobel Prize in 2006. His bank has diversified into numerous other financing ventures.[30]

- Dale Ortman began collecting repairing and distributing fishing rods to children in 2013. Based in the Pennsylvania, Dale has introduced three hundred fifty children to fishing and enjoying the outdoors. He was awarded The TODAY Show's Small Acts, Big Impacts contest sponsored by Wells Fargo, which provided him with $50,000 to continue his work.[31]

Highly sensitive people can use baby steps to create a life that suits the talents, interests, and needs of their nature. Whether working on social change, social entrepreneurial efforts like Yunus, or community actions like Dale Ortman, there is a way to start small and create a meaningful and rewarding life using baby steps.

The Before And After Tool For Problem Solving And Progress

What do you do when you do not know what to do?

This is a technique I learned from Robert Fritz, who is an accomplished musician, composer, filmmaker, and creativity expert. He has written The Path of Least Resistance, an important book about the creative process.

Robert Fritz maintains and has discovered through research that creativity is philosophically neutral. His practice of handling and mastering the creative process is independent of beliefs, ideologies, self-image, and other ideas that we think matter in the creative process. They don't.[32]

Robert Fritz has discovered through his own creativity and his examination of mastering the creative process that successful creativity requires the right structure to be effective as he describes here:

30   Wikipedia, https://en.wikipedia.org/wiki/Muhammad_Yunus

31   Wells Fargo, Small is HugeSM http://stories.wellsfargobank.com/pennsylvania-angler-wins-national-community-hero-contest/

32   Robert Fritz, The Creative Process is Philosophically Neutral, August, 2015 http://www.robertfritz.com/wp/the-creative-process-is-philosophically-neutral/

"In my book, The Path of Least Resistance, I describe two vastly different types of orientations: reactive-responsive; and creative-generative. In one orientation you either react or respond to the prevailing circumstances. In the other, you organize your life around your choices, often about your highest aspirations and deepest values. These orientations are not simply a matter of adopting a new attitude or trying on different beliefs. It is a matter of structure. In fact, people often want to make positive changes in their lives, but if the underlying structure is unchanged, all that will happen is an oscillating pattern in which there is change, but then there is a reversal that brings the person back to the original condition. This is a structural dynamic, and, like the rest of physics, is nothing personal."[33]

Robert Fritz uses and recommends a simple exercise to develop your ability to operate in a creative-generative way:

1. Imagine in your mind where you want to go or what you want to accomplish. Be as clear as possible about what you are seeking.

2. Next focus on where you are. Be honest about your current reality.

3. Now envision them both at the same time next to each other in your mind. One can be in front of the other, or they can be side by side. This part of the exercise creates a creative tension that you will want to resolve.

4. Hold them both in your mind's eye for several minutes. As you do, your mind will look for ways to connect them. You will then generate ideas for bridging your present and future state with little effort.

---

33 Robert Fritz, Thinking In Structures, August, 2015, http://www.robertfritz.com/wp/thinking-in-structures/

5. Next take what you learned from the exercise and makes plans for implementing the new ideas.

This exercise helps you focus on what you want to accomplish and removes distractions from your attention. It helps highly sensitive people when they are overwhelmed connect to what they need and want to be doing so it is a way to reclaim one's energy from overwhelm, the claims for attention made by others and ancillary considerations that have nothing to do with what you want to focus on.

Self Assertion And The Safety Of Constructive Action

There are a number of reasons why self-assertion is a challenge for highly sensitive people:

1. HSPs take in so much information that they have difficulty processing all of the information fast enough to formulate an idea of what they want and what they want to say. As a result, they are not quick on their feet when responding to others.

2. HSPs are unlikely to assert themselves when they think that the social group they are in is stacked against them. If the values of the people around them are incongruent, many highly sensitive people will not assert their needs.

3. The more adversarial or competitive the environment, the less likely HSPs are to assert themselves. Highly sensitive people are more collaborative than competitive. They stay away from combative social interaction because it is often damaging and counterproductive.

Because of these reasons, self-assertion for highly sensitive people requires different approaches:

- Highly sensitive people need to be able to process information in a way that enables them to respond more easily to others. Frameworks like the ones discussed in this book go a long way toward helping HSPs get a handle on the people and situations around them. By becoming familiar with useful frameworks like Spiral Dynamics and The Whole Self Framework of Bill Plotkin, highly sensitive people can develop realistic expectations about other people that will let them interact with greater confidence.

- HSPs want and need to relate to others from their own self-value. Because sensitivity has been devalued for so long, many highly sensitive people undervalue their gifts and natural talents. By becoming more aware of all that they offer, highly sensitive people can treat themselves as valuable and expect that from others as well.

- Being assertive means being able to state your needs and also to set boundaries. The easiest way to do both is to state your need in a way that serves other people. "I am most productive when I am able to take frequent breaks to recharge" is one example.

- Seeking a constructive way to present what you want to say makes self-assertion safe for you and others. Start by asking yourself what is the most constructive choice you could make now and let your intuition guide you. This question will lead to you a positive, constructive choice that is good for you and others. Present what you are seeking in a way that is good for the other person(s). This process puts you in a position to be gracious toward others while taking care of yourself. It also lets you be confident that you have done your best to honor yourself and others, and that is a lovely way to work and be with other people.

Self-assertion is an important skill for everyone. Highly sensitive people place important expectations on themselves. They want to have integrity and be authentic, constructive and humane. It can, therefore, take time to develop the skills in self-assertion that highly sensitive people need and desire.

The Value Of Context Driven Choices

Context is your environment. It is all of the natural, cultural, institutional elements around you. If you live in a desert, you would not build an igloo because the context is wrong for that type of building!

Context gives us clues about what is needed so we are not operating in a vacuum or just according to the whims of individuals. Context is our common ground with others so that being different does not have to limit our ability to participate in the world. Approaching your shared environment with others this way lets you focus on what you can do and what you can contribute and allows others to do the same.

Being context-oriented shifts your relating from being personality-driven and different to the task or project you are working on with others. There are many different types of contexts:

- Work

- Social

- Family

- Geographical

- Cultural

Contexts have specific requirements. Most of us do not wear a bathing suit to church or give out Valentine's candy on Halloween. We are aware of the expectation that we focus on work and not our social life when at work, and when at home that we need to focus on family, although more and more the lines are blurred between work and family.

Understanding contexts helps a highly sensitive person in a number of ways:

- Context awareness enables the highly sensitive person meet shared expectations around dress, protocol and other group behaviors and in doing so reduced the stress of social situations.

- Taking the time to learn contexts is an act of social friendship and makes it easier to be accepted by others.

- The sensitive person who prepares for the various social contexts in life reduces worries about socializing and can focus on social interaction instead.

- Understanding a social, work, or cultural context helps to make an HSP more confident and self-assured, which makes socializing more enjoyable.

Process As Bridge

Because of their energetic sensitivity, highly sensitive people are process sensitive. What this means is that highly sensitive people tune into the energetic flow around them. The deep processing of HSPs is connected to this rich energetic flow. Process sensitivity is a wonderful quality. However, the non-HSP world is more structure and goal focused.

Energy sensitivity provides HSPs with a window into both the known and the unknown. They can live at that place which I call the "next step," a place that lets us move forward in spite of uncertainty. Although handling the unknown can be challenging for anyone, HSPs have a natural energetic connection with the unknown, which makes emptiness and uncertainly less threatening.

Highly sensitive people's energy sensitivity helps them notice nuanced shifts in people, processes, and structures, so it is an important source of information about current conditions in the surrounding environment. When HSPs combine their ability to tune into process with a knowledge of frameworks like Spiral Dynamics and the Whole Self they become extremely valuable. They can offer ideas and solutions that others might not know because of their energetic, process oriented perceptions.

Energy sensitivity offers HSPs a status window like a fuel gauge in a car, but it does not give them information about the larger context of the situation they are perceiving. HSPs rightfully hesitate to jump into situations when they know that they have a limited information. Sometimes they do not have the intimate insider knowledge that can be important for realizing needed changes or the technical skills to figure out how to effect change. It can be hard for them to formulate successful strategies.

HSPs' capacity for process-oriented thinking can lead them forward in their own lives in an intelligent way. If they can create the nurturing foundation they need to be at their best, they can become a light for the value of compassion, kindness, and regard for themselves and others. A strong foundation will insulate them from the temptations of power and power-oriented individuals who may want to appropriate them for their purposes and use their empathy as a doorway for their exploitation. They can invite others into a different way and embrace them when changing to a kinder way of being. HSPs can disengage from destructive people and forces so that they can self protect without having to hide. They can create a strong foundation that offers natural self protection for themselves as they create bridges between their energetic world and the world of structure and conflict. When they create a strong foundation and good skills, they can shine as they should.

As highly sensitive people become more welcome in the world, collaboration between HSPs and non-HSPs will become easier. Anything highly sensitive people can do to encourage it will be helpful.

CHAPTER 12

The Skills We Need

The best way to start making changes is to assess which skills you have and which additional skills you need to acquire.

Essential Basic Skills

Highly sensitive people have a greater need than most for strong self-care. The following practices can provide you with the kind of self-support that lets you be in the world in a happily productive way:

- Basic daily health regimen: The right health regimen is calming, supporting, and detoxing. A regular schedule with set times for rising and sleeping, eating, and exercising is calming for the body and nervous system. When the body learns to expect healthy self-care, it becomes more available for the life you want to live.

- Regular sleep: This provides a daily release and restoration to the body to heal the nervous system. Honoring your body's need for rest will reduce stress and overwhelm.

- Diet appropriate for your body type: Food is natural intelligence for the body. What you eat directly affects the health and resilience of your cells, including your immune system.

- Strategies for handling sound and other sensitivities: Each HSP needs tools for handling specific sensitivities like sound.

- Stress relief practices like meditation: Meditation is a great way to restore the nervous system and release yourself from energetic negativity that has settled in the body.

- Exercise: This is a known mood elevator, and it relieves stress, increases metabolism, and improves your resilience.

- Medical attention for stress-related and other disorders.

- Emotional healing practices like journaling, accessing gratitude and forgiveness.

- Therapy for emotional healing, if needed.

- Doing inner work: This allows you to process feelings, accept the inner child, and reclaim your life from early conditioning.

- Energy healing practices like reiki and other forms of bodywork: They can help to release buried trauma and painful stuck energy. Bodywork helps relieve stress.

- Learning to discern who is good for you and who is not: This way, you are not allowing your energy to be used by exploitive individuals.

- Learning to be present and detached: You can avoid becoming enmeshed with others, allowing you to maintain perspective and freedom of movement in your relationships with others.

- Energy self-protection to prevent your energy from being abused and depleted by others.

- How to handle emotional differences without taking responsibility for the feelings of others.

- How to create a bridge between yourself and non-HSPs to ease acceptance and understanding so that you can work with others in a constructive way.

Physical care provides you with the physical resilience to handle your emotional and mental challenges as a highly sensitive person. Emotional healing helps free your energy of toxic, stuck feelings and the energy of others. Using your energy to work with others in an effective manner frees your mind of unnecessary anxiety.

When your foundation is weak, your energy can be spent shoring yourself up. Anxiety and self-doubt can cause you to hold back because you are fearful of making mistakes. A strong foundation helps you to see how you contribute to the world more easily so you can interact with others from a self-appreciating place. It also helps you embrace your purpose in life, which will help you feel happier and more fulfilled.

Some Helpful Advanced Skills

In addition to learning skills for handling our sensitivity, other skills support your ability to take your rightful place in the world. They include:

- learn how to identify and express the concrete benefits that your sensitive trait brings to the table so you can speak from a position of strength.

- understand the stages of human development, individual and cultural, so you can make intelligent choices with people who are in a different stage of development .

- identify where you belong. Living and working among like-minded people is healthier and energy conserving for highly sensitive people.

- identify where the people are around you evolutionally (developmentally) so you do not create anguish for yourself from unrealistic expectations.

- become smarter about which problems are yours and which belong to others so you are not taking on the responsibilities of others.

- learn to assess healthy vs. toxic situations and develop effective strategies for handling them so you do not invest in making something work that cannot.

- interact and work with others more comfortably because you know who is and is not a good fit for you, so you can adjust your relationship expectations accordingly.

- develop realistic and useful social strategies you can be confident about so that you experience more success.

- become sophisticated in using and protecting your energy sensitivity.

- accept that some people will not understand or accept highly sensitive people and have a strategy for handling it graciously.

- learn how to create space for yourself in a world that does not so you can honor your needs for self care.

- master various energy management techniques for self protection to minimize harm from the energetic dissonance of others.

- become skilled in being present and detached at the same time to create space for seeking advice from your higher self—the gracious, transpersonal part of you that is your true and best self—in social situations.

- develop awareness of the fear-based energies of oppression, domination, and competition, and how they manifest and how to handle them.

- learn to use your sensitivity to stretch your sense of possibility and the possibilities of others.

- develop a "library" of energy awareness for reference.

- learn to identify the energy in social games so you are not victimized.

- develop ways to lead in compassionate and mindful forgiveness.

- develop the skills needed to become constructive as much of the time as possible—a developmental path and a lifetime journey.

- learn what it means to be "whole" and develop your wholeness.

- learn new ways of creating bridges between yourself and others.

- become skilled at creating inclusion around you to minimize the fear of dominating group agendas.

- learn how to use frameworks to facilitate deep processing so you can access deeper levels of natural intelligence and creativity.

- learn how to create and use rituals to increase your effectiveness so you can use your limited energy for what is most important.

Once a highly sensitive person has basic needs met, life can be an interesting exploration of possibilities, ideas, and adventures. Having basic needs met reduces neediness and makes it easier to detach in social situations. It does not eliminate challenges or even the disappointment you will experience, but it will make it easier for you to separate yourself from negativity.

Being able to find more social control for yourself will open the door for you to create the life you desire.

Skills will help you become more sophisticated in coping with the situations in your life. They will help you become wise and constructive and develop your inner competence, which is enjoyable and priceless. You can celebrate your nature as you improve your life and the lives of others.

CHAPTER 13

Creating A New Highly Sensitive Life

Many highly sensitive people are accustomed to seeing their lives as limited because their natures are not suited to modern capitalism. As you now know, the world is slowly changing so there are more opportunities for highly sensitive people to participate in ways that suit them.

Revisioning Your Life As A Highly Sensitive Person

With all the possibilities available to highly sensitive people, making changes can be exciting as well as frightening.

The first step is to take a step back and consider where you are:

- Are you starting out in life or in transition from one stage of life to another?

- Are you established in a career and looking for volunteering opportunities?

- Are you looking to use you skills in an environment that matches who you are?

If you are seeking a change, one good way to evaluate your possibilities is to consider how your nature and gifts mesh with some of the change efforts taking place around the world. However, change works better when it is incremental and well thought-out. Therefore some planning is necessary.

Before you consider changes of any kind ask yourself, "Where is my stake in the ground? Where do I want to put down roots? What do I want to feed in the world?" You can find that answer by asking:

- Where is my joy? What lights me up and make me feel glad to be alive?

- Where do I feel most at home and most like myself? What types of interests are "me"?

With those two questions in mind, see what resonates for you:

- The healing fields?

- Environmental movements?

- Community efforts including Slow Money, Transition Towns and the Commons?

- An artistic path?

- Spiritual work?

- Social activism?

- A business environment?

- Social entrepreneurship?

Whatever you chose, there are possibilities. Any field has the need for a wide variety of roles and skills. If you are making a change, you can use current skills in a new environment while you develop new skills to move into a different position. You can also use experience in a field to support you while you are developing new abilities. Whatever you do, you need to consider the needs of your trait by factoring them in to your plans.

You planning should include:

1. Choosing the right environment for you:

   » Working for a company or organization

» Self employment

» Working full time or part time

2.   Taking your resources into account:

» Do you have or could you develop an expertise
that would allow you to work for yourself and at your
own pace?

» Can you plan to have your needs under control so you
have choices about how you work?

Creating A Path And A Plan

The possibilities for highly sensitive people are very encouraging. To get
started consider:

1.   1 Your personal foundation:

» Do you have your basic needs met?

» Do you have a support system in place?

» Do you have a community you can turn to?

2.   Skills

» What skills do you have?

» What formal or informal education do you have in your
desired field?

» What experience do you have, and are the skills
transferrable?

If you need to build a foundation, start there while considering what field you would like to enter. You can scout new fields and opportunities while you are strengthening your foundation. It can be fun to do!

Building a strong foundation includes developing skills. In a fast-changing world, developing skills requires basic training as well as a lifetime commitment to ongoing education. Being able to learn incrementally is perfect for a highly sensitive person.

If you need to work on your foundation, then a slower pace in changing jobs or careers might make the best choice. If you have strong resources, you may make bigger changes. If you are strong in skills and experience, your ability to create a new position, change careers, or start your own business is easier.

You need to take your sensitivity into account. The more you can take a long-term view and make changes one step at a time, the more successful you can be in creating a life you enjoy.

While you are developing a vision and a plan, take the time for improving your self-care. Most HSPs are very gifted and we need those gifts. However, it is easy to fall into the trap of deferring self-care in your eagerness to achieve your objectives. I am guilty of this myself.

I hope you will embrace your unique path and come to appreciate what you bring to the world to make it a better place. Keep in mind that becoming who you were meant to be is a lifelong task. Hopefully you are excited about your possibilities, because they are exciting.

What Is Your New Story?

One way to create a new path for yourself is to write a new story for yourself. Ask yourself:

- When you imagine your best authentic self in the world, what are you doing and being?

- How is what you want to do different from what you would like?

- What do you want to do that is similar to what you are doing now?

- What is the difference that you make or would like to make?

- How is the new evolving world syncing with your path in the past and the direction you would like to take in the future?

Answering questions like these can help you discover your truest path. You inner guides will help you if you ask for their wisdom.

Where To Find Like Minded People

Highly sensitive people have difficulty finding kindred spirits. Even HSPs who are in the HSP Facebook groups notice that each highly sensitive person is different. Sometimes the best course is to find people who mesh with your values and then find the HSPs among them. Meet-ups are great ways to find people with similar interests in your area.

Networking groups online and offline can be helpful as well. LinkedIn can be useful since many sensitive people are on it. People who are sensitive are also found in alternative health groups, and artistic or writer groups.

There are groups for all the different topics that were listed in the book. Some are in the resources section to help you get started.

CONCLUSION

This book has covered a lot of ground:

- Elaine Aron's "DOES" model, which beautifully describes the important gifts of highly sensitive people.

- Frameworks including Spiral Dynamics and the Whole Self framework of Bill Plotkin, which offer HSPs the opportunity to understand the world in a way that lets them process energy faster and in a more satisfying way.

- Capitalism and its effects on highly sensitive people.

- The new trends in culture creation around the commons, which are offering fresh opportunities for HSPs.

- The skills highly sensitive people need to become effective.

- How to get started creating a new life.

I hope you have found this book useful and that it has provided you with perspective and a new sense of hope about the future. The information here has been very helpful to me in navigating the world with my sensitivity. I am so thankful that we have new frameworks that will help highly sensitive people make better decisions to support their well-being and find their place in the world. In doing so they help us return to a right relationship with nature—our home.

I firmly believe that highly sensitive people are important right now as part of the transition to a new compassionate human world—a world that is good for all of us.

I hope I have helped you find some ideas for yourself that will make your life what you would like it to be. The resources section has many tools to help you make your way to a more satisfying life.

Best wishes for your happiness and success in the future.

RESOURCES

The resources section lists some books, websites, and articles related to the topics of the book. It is a starting point for each of the topics so that you can begin your exploration of subjects that interest you.

Courses Relates To The Book

HSP Health offers two courses specifically related to the content of this book:

1. The Whole Self course: an in-depth look at the Whole Self framework applied to the needs of highly sensitive people. It includes information, exercises, and a forum for questions and coaching.

2. The Foundation Course for Highly Sensitive People: an in-depth course that dives deep into the highly sensitive trait to claim it and reframe it. It explores culture, Spiral Dynamics,

work, relationships including fear patterns and boundaries, energy mastery, and Ayurveda. It also offers exercises, and a forum for questions and coaching.

Additional information can be found at Sensitive Evolution. http://www.sensitiveevolution.com

Highly Sensitive Trait

Research About The Highly Sensitive Trait

HSPerson HSPerson is the website of Elaine Aron, Ph.D., the psychologist whose groundbreaking book, The Highly Sensitive Person, put a name on a condition that had eluded definition. She is responsible for a lot of the research into the highly sensitive trait. Her website features her research, insights into the HSP trait, information about her books and HSP meetings, as well as many resources and a newsletter. http://www.hsperson.com/

HSP Gatherings

Lifeworks Lifeworks was founded by HSP Jacquelyn Strickland, "...a Licensed Professional Counselor, Coach and workshop leader based in Fort Collins, Colorado. She has been a certified trainer in the Myers-Briggs Personality Inventory since 1991." Jacquelyn offers a lot of information about the HSP trait and has classes online to help highly sensitive people to know themselves better. She is well known for her HSP Gatherings, which are annual tribal meetings for highly sensitive people to meet each other and learn more about the trait. http://www.lifeworkshelp.com/

Websites: Authors And Experts

HSPerson HSPerson is the website of Elaine Aron, Ph.D., the psychologist whose groundbreaking book, The Highly Sensitive Person, put a name on a condition that had eluded definition. She is responsible for a lot of the research into the highly sensitive trait. Her website features her research, insights into the HSP trait, information about her books and HSP meetings, as well as many resources and a newsletter. http://www.hsperson.com/

Dr. Judith Orloff Judith Orloff, author of Emotional Freedom, is a psychiatrist who specializes in emotional healing with an emphasis on mind-body integration and relationship management for intuitives. Dr. Orloff offers numerous articles and videos, has her own blog and contributes blogs for The Huffington Post and Psychology Today. She lectures frequently and provides many resources on her website. http://www.drjudithorloff.com/

Dr. Ted Zeff Ted Zeff is one of the most important voices for sensitive men. He is the author of The Highly Sensitive Person's Survival Guide, The Highly Sensitive Person's Companion, The Strong, Sensitive Boy, and The Power of Sensitivity: Success Stories of Highly Sensitive People Thriving in a Nonsensitive World. His site offers articles, tips, workshops, and coaching opportunities. http://drtedzeff.com/

Sensitive Evolution (formerly HSP Health) is Maria Hill's comprehensive website about health and self-actualization for highly sensitive people. It explores the characteristics and causes of the HSP trait, issues around being different, and strategies for personal development. It offers a blog, library, coaching, and online courses as well as alternative health solutions and other resources for common HSP challenges. http://www.sensitiveevolution.com/

The Highly Sensitive Person's Publishing Company Cliff Harwin helps other highly sensitive people understand themselves and their sensitivity so that they could have a more enjoyable and more successful life. He has written Making Sense Of Your High Sensitivity, and offers numerous aids for highly sensitive people. Cliff offers a variety of coaching programs to help HSPs on their path. http://www.thehighlysensitiveperson.com/

Highly Sensitive (.org) Douglas Eby is the creative force behind Highly Sensitive. He is a long-time researcher and writer about the highly sensitive trait and creativity. His websites include Talent Develop, High Ability, The Inner Actor, The Inner Writer, The Inner Entrepreneur, Women and Talent, and Depression and Creativity. He offers numerous videos and other resources on various aspects of creativity. Douglas is very active on social media. http://www.highlysensitive.org/

HSP Notes Peter Messerschmidt is one of the first bloggers to write about the highly sensitive trait; he began in 2002. He is one of several highly sensitive men who are open about their sensitivity and work to help other HSPs make to journey to acceptance and success. Peter's blog offers many insights, and is rich in resources for highly sensitive people who want to connect with others including his many websites for HSPs around the country. http://www.hspnotes.com/

Ane Axford, M.S. LMFT Ane is an HSP who has developed a counseling practice that provides a wide variety of relationship and personal counseling. Her services include: Individual, Group, and Relational Therapy; Clinical Hypnosis; Highly Sensitive Persons; Codependence to Interdependence; Chronic Health Issues–Resolving Autoimmune Disorders–Celiac Disease and Digestive Disorders, HIV/AIDS, Muscular Disorders (TMJ, Fibro, Scoliosis); ADD, ADHD, Autism Spectrum Disorder Treatment; Trauma and Phobia Release; and Sexual Abuse/Sexual Offense Treatment. http://aneaxford.com/

Lifeworks Lifeworks was founded by HSP Jacquelyn Strickland. According to her website, Jacquelyn is "...a Licensed Professional Counselor, Coach and workshop leader based in Fort Collins, Colorado. She has been a certified trainer in the Myers-Briggs Personality Inventory since 1991." Jacquelyn offers a lot of information about the HSP trait and has classes online to help highly sensitive people to know themselves better. She is well known for her HSP Gatherings, which are annual tribal meetings for highly sensitive people to meet each other and learn more about the trait. http://www.lifeworkshelp.com/

Websites: Coaches And Therapists

Lifeworks Lifeworks was founded by HSP Jacquelyn Strickland. According to her website, Jacquelyn is "...a Licensed Professional Counselor, Coach and workshop leader based in Fort Collins, Colorado. She has been a certified trainer in the Myers-Briggs Personality Inventory since 1991." Jacquelyn offers a lot of information about the HSP trait and has classes online to help highly sensitive people to know themselves better. She is well known for her HSP Gatherings, which are annual tribal meetings for highly sensitive people to meet each other and learn more about the trait. http://www.lifeworkshelp.com/

Mary Kay Parkinson HSP Mary Kay Parkinson is an energy healer and life coach based in Maryland. Her site offers information about the HSP trait, and many articles about living well as an HSP. Mary Kay is a highly trained psychologist, energy healer, and coach in spiritual development. She has a BA in Psychology, and has studied at the Barbara Brennan School of Healing, the Bert Hellinger Institute USA, The Center For Intention Living, and the Potomac Massage Training Institute. http://www.marykayparkinson.com/

Janine Ramsey is the creator or sensitivity style ™ "a model that helps people with differing levels of sensitivity live and work together harmoniously. http://www.janineramsey.com.au/

Highly Sensitive People Jim Hallowes, author of Chopped Liver for the Loving Spirit, offers a well rounded website for highly sensitive people covering the highly sensitive trait, health, relationships, career, and spirituality. Jim is a well-known HSP coach and provides many resources to facilitate the healing and growth of HSPs. http://www.highlysensitivepeople.com/

Kathryn Nulf is a certified health coach and registered yoga teacher, who supports HSPs in her private and group coaching programs to step out of overwhelm and finally feel free and at peace around food. Her passion is to help HSPs discover what it's like to have an inner flame so strong that it's not swayed by every stressful event in life. Kathryn helps her clients embrace their unique trait so that their whole self can embrace life. http://www.litfromwithinwellness.com/

Kate Stefans understands how easy it is to get completely lost in the depth of all that we feel and fall into addictions to cope with this depth. She understands food, thoughts, and control. Knowing this, she works to guide HSPs to a place of healing, a place of perceiving the vastness of all they are so that they may contribute to the world with their incredible complexity. You can find her at http://katestefans.com/.

Sheep Dressed Like Wolves Andy Mort is a musician, songwriter and pod-caster who has established a community for highly sensitive creatives to support their success. http://www.sheepdressedlikewolves.com/

Other HSP Resources:

Sensitive Person Thomas Eldridge's Sensitive Person website has many articles about the highly sensitive trait and how to handle it. His site is a go-to website for resources of all kinds for people learning about the HSP trait and seeking ways to handle their different nature. http://www.sensitiveperson.com/

Sally Gage has created a website in honor of her highly sensitive son, Ben, who died of a rare illness. She is dedicating her time to helping highly sensitive children. She can be found at http://www.highlysensitivekids.com.au/

The Highly Sensitive Family is a comprehensive website about and for the highly sensitive family rich in resources related to the highly sensitive trait, stress and health and the needs of highly sensitive children. It can be reached at http://www.thehighlysensitivefamily.wordpress.com/

Books

The Highly Sensitive Person by Dr. Elaine Aron

The Highly Sensitive Person is the 1996 groundbreaking book in which Dr. Elaine Aron describes the nature of the little-understood highly sensitive person. It provides insight into what it means to be highly sensitive and how it affects childhood, work, and relationships. The book offers many tips for HSPs seeking strategies on how to deal with their sensitivity.

The Highly Sensitive Person in Love: Understanding and Managing Relationships When the World Overwhelms You by Dr. Elaine Aron

"Based on Elaine N. Aron's groundbreaking research on temperament and intimacy, The Highly Sensitive Person in Love offers practical help for highly sensitive people seeking happier, healthier romantic relationships.

From low-stress fighting to sensitive sexuality, the book offers a wealth of practical advice on making the most of all personality combinations. Complete with illuminating self-tests and the results of the first survey ever done on sex and temperament, The Highly Sensitive Person in Love will help you discover a better way of living and loving." Excerpt from Amazon

The Highly Sensitive Child by Dr. Elaine Aron

This book by Dr. Aron explains the challenges of being and parenting a highly sensitive child. It discusses the misunderstanding that many highly sensitive children experience and offers tips and strategies to help a highly sensitive child become healthy and strong.

The Highly Sensitive Person's Survival Guide: Essential Skills for Living Well in an Overstimulating World By Dr. Ted Zeff

Dr. Ted Zeff tackles the practical issues around sensitive living in this comprehensive guide for handling the highly sensitive trait. The book includes tips for handling stress, distractions, and relationships, and offers a variety of stress reduction strategies. It is one of the most important books for handling sensitivity.

The Strong Sensitive Boy by Dr. Ted Zeff

"In this groundbreaking book, psychologist Ted Zeff explores the unique challenges of sensitive boys, showing parents, educators, and mentors how to help sensitive boys grow into strong, happy, and confident men. Dr. Zeff offers practical advice on how to help your son increase his self-esteem and thrive in the family, at school, with friends, and in sports." Excerpt from Amazon

The Power Of Sensitivity by Dr. Ted Zeff

"Dr. Ted Zeff has compiled 43 uplifting success stories, submitted from highly sensitive people from 10 different countries. These triumphs are shared here to help the international HSP community learn new ways to manage their trait and thrive in our non-sensitive world. Sit back and enjoy reading these delightful and inspiring stories from HSPs around the world, as you learn new methods to empower yourself." Excerpt from Amazon

Emotional Freedom: Liberate Yourself from Negative Emotions and Transform Your Life by Judith Orloff, MD

Judith Orloff is a master of energy and therefore a wonderful source for highly sensitive people. She is an MD who has written a number of books, including this bestseller, providing information into energy toxicity and relationships and how to change yourself so that you can let go of the negativity in the world. She is one of the most important writers about sensitivity and emotional health and a must read for highly sensitive people.

Making Work Work For The Highly Sensitive Person by Barrie Jaeger

This book redefines work to suit the highly sensitive person. Barrie breaks down work into three categories: Drudgery, Craft, and Calling, and explains what each is and how they affect highly sensitive people. She offers numerous insights for sensitives who want to be more effective in their lives.

Real World Advice Specifically For Highly Sensitive People By Cliff Harwin

Cliff Harwin explores the many ways that highly sensitive people are challenged and offers practical advice for all areas of life. He writes in an approachable, down-to-earth style that makes his substantial advice very accessible.

Finely Tuned: How To Thrive As A Highly Sensitive Person or Empath by Barrie Davenport

Barrie Davenport is a coach who has written this book for highly sensitive people who are tired of being misunderstood and want to take charge of their lives.

Quiet: The Power of Introverts in a World That Can't Stop Talking by Susan Cain

Susan's bestselling book, Quiet: The Power of Introverts in a World That Can't Stop Talking, captures the essence of being introverted and the differences between extroverts and introverts. Her book is an especially useful window into the work life of an introvert. Susan's site has many resources for introverts.

http://www.quietrev.com/

Frameworks

Spiral Dynamics is one of the frameworks discussed in this book. Spiral Dynamics.org is the organization of Chris Cowan, one of the authors of the book, Spiral Dynamics. He offers a lot of great information on the website as well as a training schedule for those wanting to learn more about Spiral Dynamics.

http://www.spiraldynamics.org/

Spiral Dynamics by Chris Cowan and Donald Beck. "Spiral Dynamics reveals the hidden codes that shape human nature, create global diversities, and drive evolutionary change. These magnetic forces attract and repel individuals, form the webs that connect people within organizations, and forge the rise and fall of nations and cultures. This book tracks our historic emergence from clans to tribes to networks and holograms; identifies seven Variations on Change, and adds power and precision to the design of human systems and 21st century leadership." Excerpt from the back cover.

Animas Valley Institute: Psychologist Bill Plotkin has written numerous books about soul-centered living and the whole self, another framework discussed in this book. He has pioneered the nature-based approach to human development and developed numerous programs to help people integrate the information into their lives. His books and programs can be found here. http://www.animas.org/

Nature and the Human Soul: Cultivating Wholeness and Community in a Fragmented World by Bill Plotkin, PH.D. Dr. Plotkin has written a guide for people seeking deeper purpose and relationship to life beyond consumer culture. He maps our development to developmental processes based in nature. In doing so he helps the reader discover their natural connection with the world and all of life so that they can develop a mature ecologically sound self that offers inner and outer satisfaction.

Wild Mind by Bill Plotkin. "Our human psyches possess astonishing resources that wait within us, but we might not even know they exist until we discover how to access them and cultivate their powers, their untapped potentials and depths. Wild Mind identifies these resources — which Bill Plotkin calls the four facets of the Self, or the four dimensions of our innate human wholeness — and also the four sets of fragmented or wounded subpersonalities that form during childhood. Rather than proposing ways to eliminate our subpersonalities (which is not possible) or to beat them into submission, Plotkin describes how to cultivate the four facets of the Self and discover the gifts of our subpersonalities. The key to reclaiming our original wholeness is not merely to suppress psychological symptoms, recover from addictions and trauma, or manage stress but rather to fully embody our multifaceted wild minds, commit ourselves to the largest, soul-infused story we're capable of living, and serve the greater Earth community." Excerpt from Amazon

Trends And Opportunities

Commons Movement
New Society Publishers is a solutions-oriented publisher providing cutting edge information, inspiration, and practical tools for change. http://www.newsociety.com/

On The Commons "On the Commons (OTC) is a commons movement strategy center founded in 2001..." Its purpose is to create a commons-based human world to replace the market based system currently in place. http://www.onthecommons.org/

Wikipedia https://en.wikipedia.org/wiki/Commons   Wikipedia has an excellent page, which offers a history of the commons as well as a list of important current leaders of this movement.

The New Economy Coalition The New Economy coalition is an umbrella organization for the many organizations working to create a commons framework. http://neweconomy.net/

"The Quiet Realization of Ivan Illich's Ideas in the Contemporary Commons Movement" by David Bollier, is a great article by David Bollier on his blog about the nature and history of the commons. http://bollier.org/blog/quiet-realization-ivan-illichs-ideas-contemporary-commons-movement

"Year One Of The Commons Movement" is an excellent discussion about the commons movement. http://www.resilience.org/stories/2011-02-16/commons-marginalized-rediscovered-year-one-global-commons-movement

"The Global Commons Movement Is Gathering Again" is a great article about the issues that the commons addresses. http://commonsrising.ning.com/forum/topics/the-global-commons-movement-is-gathering-again

Relocalization Resources
Post Carbon Institute is one of the most important websites about transitioning to a post carbon future. http://www.postcarbon.org/relocalize/

Transition Network is an online network of people creating "transition towns," establishing post carbon sustainable communities. https://www.transitionnetwork.org/

Transition Culture is a blog about creating a new transition culture. https://www.transitionnetwork.org/blogs/rob-hopkins

The Slow Movement: Quality Over Quantity
Wikipedia Slow Movement is a comprehensive resource on the Slow Movement. It offers a history as well as information and resources for many different spheres of Slow Movement activity. https://en.wikipedia.org/wiki/Slow_Movement

Slow Food USA, "… is part of the global Slow Food network of over 100,000 members in more than 150 countries. Through a vast volunteer network of local chapters, youth and food communities, we link the pleasures of the table with a commitment to protect the community, culture, knowledge and environment that make this pleasure possible."

https://www.slowfoodusa.org/

Slow Food International is the international grass roots organization of millions of people in one hundred fifty countries, promoting healthy clean food for all. http://www.slowfood.com/

Slow Money is an organization to fund local farming and restore food balance. https://slowmoney.org/

Social Alterations is a learning hub for sustainable fashion. http://social-alterations.com/

Quality Health Care, NJ Biz, an article about the quality movement in health care. http://www.njbiz.com/article/20141023/NJBIZ01/141029875/federal-government-joins-qualityoverquantity-health-care-movement-with-840m-grant-program

In Praise Of Slowness, by Carl Honore, is a book that questions the fascination of speed in favor of sane paced living and doing. http://www.carlhonore.com/books/in-praise-of-slowness/

The Craft Of Use, Centre For Sustainable Fashion, is a hub for sustainable fashion. http://www.craftofuse.org/

Connected World: The Rise Of The Amateur And The Maker Movement

The Rise Of The Maker Movement, P2P Foundation, is an article that discusses the new Maker Movement and how more and more people will earn their living from what they make. http://p2pfoundation.net/Maker_Movement

The Rise Of The "Professional Amateur" And The Fall Of Gated, Exclusionary "Clubs," TechDirt, an article that discusses gatekeeping in its various forms and how it is going away. https://www.techdirt.com/articles/20120201/0931161762   2/rise-professional-amateur-fall-gated-exclusionary-clubs.shtml

Social Entrepreneurship

The New Heroes, What Is Social Entrepreneurship, is a video that explains social entrepreneurship. http://www.pbs.org/opb/thenewheroes/whatis/

Wikipedia—Social Entrepreneurship, https://en.wikipedia.org/wiki/Social_entrepreneurship

Social Velocity is a website that supports nonprofit social entrepreneurs so that they can be more effective. http://www.socialvelocity.net/

Skoll Foundation is an umbrella organization for the many social entrepreneurship missions of Skoll, one of the most important organizations in the social entrepreneurship space. http://www.newsociety.com/

Skoll World Forum For Social Entrepreneurship is an annual forum for social entrepreneurship leaders. http://skollworldforum.org/

What Is Social Enterprise? A Social Enterprise Alliance article about business designed to serve the common good. https://www.se-alliance.org/what-is-social-enterprise

Reshaping Capitalism: The Sharing Movement

The New Economy Coalition is a website for organizations creating a new economic framework that focuses on increased sharing. http://new-economy.net/

Shareable is a news information, action, and connection hub for the sharing movement. http://www.shareable.net/

Compassionate Cities And Equity Movements

The Charter for Compassion is a website about the efforts and partnerships of the organization to create compassionate collaborative actions around the globe. http://charterforcompassion.org/cities

Compassionate Cities is a website dedicated to compassionate initiatives around the world. http://www.compassionatecities.org/

Creativity

Robert Fritz is a composer, filmmaker, and organizational consultant. He is the founder of **Robert Fritz** Inc. and author of the international bestseller The Path of Least Resistance. http://www.robertfritz.com/wp/

Eric Maisel is the author of more than forty books. His interests include creativity, the creative life, and the field of creativity coaching which he founded. http://www.ericmaisel.com

Julia Cameron/Artist's Way Julia Cameron wrote the Artist's Way in 2002 to help people learn about and engage with their own creative process. The book is an international bestseller. Her website also offers a course on the creative process. http://juliacameronlive.com/

Douglas Eby is a California-based psychologist who specializes in creativity and the highly sensitive person. His websites are packed with information and insights for the highly sensitive creative. http://talentdevelop.com/

Andrew Mort is a London-based musician and songwriter with a website for creative introverts http://www.sheepdressedlikewolves.com/

Skills

Boundaries

Boundaries in Human Relationships: How to Be Separate and Connected by Anne Linden is a well thought-out book on boundaries. It is especially helpful for highly sensitive people because Anne has created a structure for understanding different types of boundaries and how to use them. Anne Linden was an actor who became a psychotherapist and founded the New York Training Institute for NLP and the NLP Center for Psychotherapy, the first of their kind in the world.

Health

Health: Ayurveda

Perfect Health is an excellent book on creating health through Ayurveda by Deepak Chopra. It describes the basics of Ayurveda and the quantum basis of Ayurvedic healing. It is very accessible and a great start for learning about Ayurveda.

Ayurvedic Experts

Dr. Vasant Lad, Ayurvedic Institute, Albuquerque, N.M.

Vasant Lad is one of the most important Ayurvedic doctors in the United States. He has bachelor and master degrees in Ayurveda from Pune University College of Ayurvedic and held important positions in Ayurvedic. In 1984, he became founder of The Ayurvedic Institute in New Mexico. Vasant Lad is the author of eleven books on Ayurveda as well as many other writings. His work has been translated into more than twenty languages. https://www.ayurveda.com/

Dr. Mark Halpern, California College of Ayurveda, Los Angeles, C.A.

Dr. Halpern is one of the few Westerners held in high regard in the Ayurvedic Medical community in the U.S. and India. Not only is he an accomplished doctor (he received the All India Award for Best Ayurvedic Physician), he also co-founded of the National Ayurvedic Medical Association, the California Association of Ayurvedic Medicine, and the National Council on Ayurvedic Education. Dr. Halpern has written two textbooks and many articles and made numerous appearances about Ayurveda. http://www.ayurvedacollege.com/

Dr. Nancy Lonsdorf, Fairfeld, I.A.

Dr. Lonsdorf is an MD trained at Johns Hopkins in Western Medicine and India and Europe in Ayurvedic medicine. She has authored several books and received the Atreya Award for Excellence in Ayurveda Practice. She is on the Planning Team for the College of Perfect Health at Maharishi University and a contributing editor for Natural Solutions formerly called Alternative Medicine. She is regarded as one of the most important Ayurvedic physicians in the United States. http://drlonsdorf.com/

Dr. Deepak Chopra, Chopra Center, Carlsbad, C.A.

Dr. Chopra is a board certified physician in Massachusetts with a specialty in Endocrinology. He was the director of New England Memorial Hospital in Stoneham, M.A. and taught at Tufts University, Boston University, and Harvard University. He founded the American Association of Ayurvedic Medicine, was one of the founders of Maharishi Ayur-Veda Products International, and became medical director of the Maharishi Ayur-Veda Health Center in Lancaster, Massachusetts. Eventually he left to start the Chopra Center, which has grown to become an important health education center in California. http://www.chopra.com

Dr. Kumuda Reddy, College Park, M.D.

Dr. Reddy is an MD and former faculty member of Albany Medical College and was the Medical Director of the Maharishi Vedic Center in Bethesda, Maryland. Dr. Reddy is an experienced practitioner of Maharishi Vedic

Medicine and an expert in family health care and presently in private practice in Bethesda, Maryland. She is also the author of a number of Ayurvedic remedy books including: Forever Healthy: An Introduction to Maharishi Ayur-Veda Health Care, For a Blissful Baby: Healthy and Happy Pregnancy with Maharishi Vedic Medicine, and Conquering Chronic Disease with Maharishi Vedic Medicine. http://www.samhita.com/

Stress

Meditation

Transcendental Meditation is a mantra-based meditation technique practiced twice a day. It is a simple technique that many highly sensitive people use for stress management. http://www.tm.org/

Fragrant Heart offers meditation tracks by categories, with lots of different styles. Each meditation is available with or without background music. Some tracks are for beginners, and they also provide a free five-day guided meditation course, daily meditations, and an app. http://www.fragrantheart.com/

Tara Brach has a large number of audio meditations covering a wide variety of topics. She has an e-book on how to meditate and offers meditations in Spanish and other languages. http://www.tarabrach.com/audioarchives-guided-meditations.html

Meditation Oasis offers a large number of guided meditations and music for meditating, an online course on how to meditate, and apps for most handheld devices. http://www.meditationoasis.com/

Journaling

750 Words is an free online journal based on Julia Cameron's journaling recommendation in her creativity course, The Artist's Way. http://750words.com/

Penzu is a totally private online diary service. http://www/penzu.com

Emotional Healing

Dr. Judith Orloff is a board-certified psychiatrist and an assistant professor of psychiatry at the University of California, Los Angeles. She has been writing and teaching about energy, health, and the mind-body connection for decades. She has written the bestseller The Ecstasy of Surrender: 12 Surprising Ways Letting Go Can Empower Your Life and Emotional Freedom. She also offers courses on her website. She has written in most major publications and appeared on Oprah and other shows. She is a popular teacher and was voted "Most Inspirational Person" for the Readers' Choice 2012 awards on About.com. http://www.drjudithorloff.com

The Daily OM was co-founded by Madisyn Taylor who is its editor-in-chief; she is responsible for all its content. Madisyn is a highly sensitive person featured in Sensitive The Movie. Madisyn has more than fifteen years experience in alternative healing methods. She features many well-known healers on her website, which offers numerous affordable healing courses. http://www.dailyom.com

In addition to meditation, journaling, and good health care, there are some other healing techniques that promote emotional healing:

EFT – Emotional Freedom Technique

EFT Universe is based on founder Gary Craig's teachings and is supported by some major healing experts. EFT may be helpful to those HSPs who suffer from the stress of negative memories. http://www.eftuniverse.com/

Acupuncture

Acupuncture is an old, well-established health modality, with many practitioners in the United States. Acupuncture uses thin needles to penetrate the skin to stimulate energy points. It is popular as a treatment for pain and fibromyalgia, which may make it in some instances a great choice for HSPs seeking pain relief. State associations, as well as accredited acupuncture schools, can be sources of competent acupuncture practitioners. The National Center for Complementary and Alternative Medicine at NIH offers a good introduction of acupuncture. http://nccam.nih.gov/health/acupuncture/

Acupressure

Acupressure is similar to acupuncture in some ways. Acupressure uses the fingers to gradually press key healing points, which stimulate the body and create healing. Acupressure treats stress-related conditions and, like reiki, can be self-administered. The acupressure.com website offers good resources. http://www.acupressure.com/

Reiki

Reiki is becoming one of the most popular forms of energy healing. It is a hands-on healing method where a practitioner places their hands on the body of a client to transfer healing energy to the body. A good introduction is available from the National Center for Complementary and Alternative Medicine at the National Institutes of Health in Bethesda, Maryland. http://nccam.nih.gov/health/reiki/D315_BKG.pdf

Karuna Reiki There are many variations on the foundational Usui Reiki. The most well known is William Rand's Karuna Reiki. His website offers this introduction: http://www.reiki.org/karunareiki/karunahomepage.html

Health: Exercise

The Walking Site is a good website for walking. It offers a very easy to use navigation system and complete basic information. http://www.thewalkingsite.com/

Wendy Bumgardner has another helpful website for walking. She is a certified marathon coach and a Ledi Nordic Walking Instructor. http://walking.about.com/

Map My Walk, is a beautiful site for people who are interested in social walking. http://www.mapmywalk.com/

Chi Walking is an interesting walking program that is designed to use the biomechanics of the body to enable the exerciser to achieve fitness with the least amount of effort and still achieve a quality result. Because of this approach, it may be an excellent choice for HSPs. http://www.chiwalking.com

Health: Yoga

Yoga is a centuries-old form of exercise that can be very gentle or very demanding, and along with walking, the exercise of choice of Ayurveda. Yoga, because it trains the body and the mind, is an excellent form of exercise.

There are many schools of yoga, which include hatha, a gentle and popular form of yoga; vinyasa or breath synchronized yoga; kundalini yoga, which works with body's chakras or energy centers; and newer forms such as the demanding power yoga.

Here are a few yoga resources to kick-start your investigation of this great form of self-care:

- **Yoga Journal** is the premier yoga magazine and a great resource for all things yoga. http://www.yogajournal.com/

- **A2ZYoga** is a great website for beginners or explorers covering all the different types of yoga and what they can do for you under their FAQs. http://www.a2zyoga.com/

- **The Yoga Site** has resources, directories, and some good articles. http://www.yogasite.com/

Exercise: NIA

The new and increasingly popular NIA is designed to make exercise natural easy and fun. It is an amazingly complete system of exercises designed for total body fitness as well as mind-body integration.

It integrates the healing practices of yoga, Alexander Technique, and Feldenkreis; the martial arts disciplines of tai chi, tae kwon do, and aikido; and the modern, Duncan, and jazz dance modalities. https://nianow.com/

Inspirational Healing

Hay House was founded by Louise Hay in 1984 to self publish her two bestselling books: Heal Your Body and You Can Heal Your Life. Since then, it has grown into one of the most important self-help resources with important self-help authors offering books and online programs. Wayne Dyer, Gregg Braden, Doreen Virtue, and Bruce Lipton are just some of the experts that offer their knowledge through Hay House. http://www.hayhouse.com/

The Daily OM was co-founded by Madisyn Taylor who is its editor-in-chief; she is responsible for all its content. Madisyn is a highly sensitive person featured in Sensitive The Movie. Madisyn has more than fifteen years experience in alternative healing methods. She features many well-known healers on her website, which offers numerous affordable healing courses. http://www.dailyom.com

Mindvalley Academy is a platform that helps spiritual teachers educate. Eckhart Tolle and Wayne Dyer are just two teachers who offer courses. It has launched a school for the soul called Soulvana and for seven years has made WorldBlu's list of Most Democratic Workplaces. http://mindvalleyacademy.com/courses

Basic And Advanced Skills

The basic and advanced skills can be found in the Foundation Course For Highly Sensitive People on the Sensitive Evolution http://www.sensitiveevolution.com